Julia C. R. Dorr

The Flower of England's Face

Julia C. R. Dorr

The Flower of England's Face

ISBN/EAN: 9783337209452

Printed in Europe, USA, Canada, Australia, Japan

Cover: Foto ©Andreas Hilbeck / pixelio.de

More available books at **www.hansebooks.com**

"THE FLOWER OF ENGLAND'S FACE"

Sketches of English Travel

BY

JULIA C. R. DORR

AUTHOR OF "FRIAR ANSELMO," "AFTERNOON SONGS," ETC., ETC.

New York
MACMILLAN AND COMPANY
AND LONDON
1895

1895,
By MACMILLAN AND CO.

Norwood Press
J. S. Cushing & Co. — Berwick & Smith
Norwood Mass. U.S.A.

TO
Katharine Keith

"Fortasse haec olim tibi juvabit meminisse"

CONTENTS.

CHAP.		PAGE
I.	A WEEK IN WALES	1
II.	BANBURY CAKES AND THE ISLE OF WIGHT	46
III.	A DAY OF CONTRASTS	70
IV.	IN THE FOREST OF ARDEN	89
V.	AT THE PEACOCK INN	126
VI.	AT HAWORTH	143
VII.	FROM THE BORDER TO INVERNESS	180
VIII.	TO CAWDOR CASTLE AND CULLODEN MOOR	209
IX.	AN ENCHANTED DAY	236

"THE FLOWER OF ENGLAND'S FACE."

I.

A WEEK IN WALES.

SHOULD it be the English Lakes, or North Wales? We were in Chester, and it was the week of the Queen's Jubilee. London was not to be thought of. To-morrow would be the great day itself, and even this staid old town, with its historic walls and towers, its queer "Rows," of which no description can convey an adequate idea, its picturesque streets and ancient houses, was alive with pleasant turmoil and excitement.

That night, at twenty minutes to ten, I stood at my window in the Grosvenor, looking up at the dark spires of the cathedral. There was no moon and the street lamps were not yet lighted, nor were my candles. Yet I found by actual experiment that I could read common newspaper print with perfect ease. Such is the length of the English twilight.

There was little sleep for Chester that night. Eastgate Street, and doubtless all the other streets, were alive with surging crowds, shouting and cheering, and singing Jubilee songs. "God save the Queen! God save the Queen!" was the burden of them all. Jubilee cakes and Jubilee candies filled the shop-windows, to say nothing of flags, medals, and souvenirs of all sorts, from a pin-cushion to a diadem. The Queen's plain, matronly face greeted one at every turn, generally rising above the black robes she most affects, lightened only by the blue ribbon of the Garter. But occasionally might be seen a more ambitious attempt at portraying the splendours of royalty. Imagine her Majesty in a bright red gown, crowned and bejewelled to the last degree!

Towards morning Chester went to bed, and we fell asleep, only to be awakened at dawn by the chiming of the cathedral bells, almost in front of our windows. It was worth waking for, — to lie there in a half-dream, and hear the liquid music soar, and swell, and die away, at last, in strains too sweet for earth. In the afternoon there was a Jubilee service for the children, for which tickets were kindly sent us. Chester is one of the smaller cathedrals; yet on that occasion, though only the south transept was used, it was said that seven thousand children and many grown people were seated in its wide spaces. Perhaps it should be stated that this transept is exceptionally large — nearly as large as the nave itself — and is known as the church of St. Oswald. The children did most of the singing, led by the trained choir and the great organ; and when the full chorus of fresh young voices rolled out grandly in the hymn, —

> "Like a mighty army
> Moves the church of God;
> Brothers, we are treading
> Where the saints have trod,"

the effect was overpowering. It would have been overwhelming anywhere, that mighty river of song; but there, in that hoary cathedral, whose vaulted aisles had echoed with the sound of prayer and psalm for twelve hundred years, it was as resistless as the waves of the ocean. "Where the saints have trod"? Were they saints, those old monks? Not all of them. They were men of like frailties with ourselves; and the good and bad mingled in monastery walls, in what we call the dark ages, as in city streets to-day. But there were grand and saintly souls among them, who laboured zealously, according to their light, for God and man. We had paced their cloisters, treading in the very imprints of their feet. We had loitered in their green, secluded closes. We had listened for the lingering cadence of their laughter in the vaulted Monk's Parlour, and in the chapter-house we had touched reverently the books they read and the missals from which they prayed. We had looked down the long, narrow vista of the scriptorium. Here, hour after hour, had the cowled heads bent over the parchment books the deft hands were illuminating with such fine tracery of leaf and flower. Perhaps the very ivies that were casting such flickering shadows on its gray arches were the direct descendants of those that dallied with " the winds that blew a thousand years ago." Who could deny it? We had wandered through the murky crypt where their ashes lie; and one of us had found, with the aid of the verger, the initials of an old fourteenth-century abbot, S. R., entwined in the foliage of one of the carved capitals in the nave, — said abbot being, according to tradition, a far-off kinsman of her own. Afterwards, she was shown reverently, in one of the cloisters, a blackened, mutilated slab that had once covered his grave or coffin, on which the S. R. appeared again, cleanly cut, as if fresh from the graver's hand.

Charles Kingsley was for some years a canon of Chester, and the friendly vergers had many stories to tell of him and his doings. It was for his sake, in part, that we planned to go in a row-boat to Eaton Hall, thinking that perhaps we, as well as the boatmen, might still hear his Mary

"call the cattle home
Across the sands o' Dee."

All the rest of the folk who wished to shun London till the hurly-burly of the Jubilee was over seemed to be going to the Lakes. So Saint Katharine and I decided on North Wales, thus avoiding the whole crowd of tourists. Conway being our first objective point, we took the Chester and Holyhead section of the London and Northwestern Railway, which runs along the shores of the river Dee and the Irish Sea, of which, in fact, the river is itself an arm. The glimpses of scenery to be caught from the flying train are exquisitely picturesque; and we two lone women could not quite control our expressions of pleasure, even though a dignified Welsh gentleman sat at the other end of the compartment, absorbed in a newspaper. Now occurred one of the small delights of travel that it is so pleasant to recall afterwards; and once again we were compelled to congratulate ourselves on having chosen the sociable and friendly rep of the second class car, rather than the more exclusive plush of the first. Our fellow passenger laid down The Times.

"I see you are interested in our Welsh scenery, ladies," he said. "Pray exchange seats with me. The views from this side are much the finer, and it is all an old story to me."

An intelligent man is really a much more interesting travelling companion than the very best guide-book; especially when he is good enough to show you a thousand points of interest, — little things that the guide-book grandly ignores, or that you would be sure not to recognize in the hurry of the moment. If it had not been for our new friend, we should hardly have noticed the chimneys of Hawarden, or strained our eyes in the attempt to see the house itself, hidden in its nest of greenery. But we did see the unpretentious parish church where Mr. Gladstone often reads the service, to the edification of himself and others. If it had not been for our friend, too, we should have had occasion to go lamenting all the rest of our days that we had passed without knowing it the ruins of Flint Castle, where Richard held the memorable interview with Bolingbroke, and sighed to be "great as his grief, or lesser than his name." It stands, what there is left of it, on a rugged hill, through which we swept in a tunnel, so that "the rude ribs of that ancient castle" were directly over our heads, and its "tattered battlements" loomed above us as we emerged into the sunlight again. The ruins of feudal castles that meet one at every turn in Wales are patent reminders that the whole land was long a bone of contention between two rival nations, and that here, time after time and generation after generation, the English kings summoned their men-at-arms in a vain attempt to subdue the valorous Welsh, secure in their mountain fastnesses. But the stronger won at last. Beautiful indeed was Gwrrych Castle that afternoon, in its setting of emerald woods, — a stately pile of cream-coloured stone, with many towers and turrets, and a mountain for a background. It is a human habitation, not a ruin, and belongs to the Marquis of Mostyn. Very near it is Abergele, once the home of Mrs. Hemans.

Modern "culture" does not thoroughly approve her of whom her greater sister in song, Mrs. Browning, said, "she never wronged that mystic breath, which breathed in all her being." But those of us who are old enough to remember the days when it was allowable to read and admire her, cannot fail to have noticed the strong hold Welsh history and Welsh legends had upon her imagination.

At Old Colwyn, "our Welsh friend," as we like to call him, having no other name to know him by, pointed out to us his own home on the hillside, divided with us a great bunch of white carnations he was carrying to his wife, shook hands with us cordially, and departed, smiling and lifting his hat as he vanished round the corner. How easy it is to do kindly things, if one only wants to!

Soon we rolled into what we more than once heard called the "stupid" town of Conway. The omnipresent porter took our luggage, and we walked a short distance to the Castle Hotel.

Conway is headquarters for the Royal Cambrian Society of Art. We wondered if that fact, or its having a landlady of artistic proclivities, accounted for the pictures, mostly oil-paintings, which covered the walls of our inn. The coffee-room and halls were lined with them, and the chambers held the overflow. In our hostess's private parlour, Kensington embroidery, old china, painted door-panels, painted milking-stools, etc., had a strangely familiar air, showing that Wales, like America, is in the march of progress. If we could only have found a decorated rolling-pin, we should have been happy. But in a conspicuous place hung two or three sketches of American scenery by Thomas Moran, sent to our hostess, as she was proud to say, by the artist himself, who had been for weeks a guest of the house. One morning, when we went down to breakfast, we found in the coffee-room an old gentleman and his wife: she, a tall, angular person, with her hair combed low on her cheeks, and then carried up over her ears, a huge cap with purple ribbons, and a gown that looked like a fifty-year-old fashion-plate; he, a curious figure that might have stepped bodily out of one of Dickens's illustrated pages. He was prowling about the room with an eyeglass, grumbling because his breakfast was not served, and venting his spleen upon those unfortunate pictures. "Abominable! Atrocious!" he kept exclaiming with a snort. "And I suppose, my dear, there are people who call this *art!*" But why need he have given the things so much attention? It is well to know when to shut one's eyes. There were lovely flowers on the table. for which he had neither glance nor word.

The thing we had come to Conway to see was the castle. But on the principle of leaving the best till the last, we saw everything else first, keeping it and gloating over it as a child gloats over his sugar-plums, though it was always in our thoughts as in our sight, — the one dominant feature in the landscape, ruling it as a mountain rules the valley.

"Be sure to go up the river to Trefriw," our friend of the carnations had said, as a parting injunction. The next morning was hot, and the cool breeze from the river was delicious. What time could be better than the present? So to the dock we went, and for an hour awaited the arrival of the small steamer; the Conway being a tidal river, and completely ruled by the caprices of the lady moon.

But we were off at last, like a parcel of children playing at sea-going, in a toy boat on a toy river. Nothing more enjoyable can well be conceived. All was so sweet, so still, so serene, that it was like moving in a happy dream. The softly rounded hills, cultivated, and clothed to their summits with all imaginable shades of green and olive; the lovely stone cottages, picturesque on the outside at least, springing up in all sorts of out-of-the-way places, — now clinging to some sharply defined point far up the hillsides, now nestling deep in sheltered valleys, but all alike mantled with ivy and bright with roses; the fern-clad banks of the stream; the arched bridges; the ancestral farmhouses, gray with age; and here and there the stately splendour of hall or castle, made a series of pictures never to be forgotten. Our captain was very accommodating, and helped to carry out the illusion that it was all play. If he saw a would-be passenger strolling leisurely over the fields towards the river, he quietly turned his prow to the shore, and waited till the new-comer leaped on board. If a woman wanted to land where there was no dock, that she might shorten the distance homewards by going " 'cross lots," she had only to suggest it, and she was put ashore forthwith, — sometimes, as it seemed, at the imminent risk of an overturn. At Trefriw, which certainly had very little to show for itself except its ferns and its long ranks of pink and purple foxgloves, there was time for luncheon, if anybody wanted it. Beyond this point the river is not navigable, and we were soon on our return voyage, "going out with the tide." The little Conway was famous for its pearl fisheries even before the Roman Conquest, and Wales boasts that a Conway pearl is one of the ornaments of the English crown to-day.

Near the head of High Street stands the Plas Mawr, or Great Mansion, built more than three centuries ago by one Robert Wynne. Its chief claim to distinction lies in the fact that its owner had the honour of entertaining Queen Elizabeth for some days. The old house is just as it was then, save for the ravages of time, which are many. But the great courts, the floors, the wood-work of panelled oak now black as ebony, the window-sashes, the small diamond-shaped panes of greenish glass, the fireplaces, and the stairways, remain unaltered, for the most part. The Plas Mawr was freshly decorated and adorned for the reception of the queen, and the letters E. R., Elizabeth Regina, appear over and over again, both in wood-carvings and on the ceilings, in connection with the royal crest. The ceilings have been barbarously whitewashed, but they must have been very beautiful when they shone in green and gold, with rich emblazonry of heraldic colours. In the great banqueting-hall — people seem never to have eaten, but always to have banqueted, in those days — are the identical tables and chairs of massive oak used by the royal party. We entered the private drawing-room of the queen, and her bed-chamber; and tried to imagine her, in the prime of her haughty womanhood, sitting in a low chair before the broad fireplace, dreaming, perhaps, of the very lovers whom she spurned. But nothing brought back the romance of the past so vividly as when our escort, the secretary of the above-named art society, said, throwing open another door, "The Earl of Leicester was in attendance upon her majesty. This was his chamber." If so, at this small, deep, diamond-paned lattice he must often have stood, as he buckled on his sword or arranged his slashed doublet. Were his thoughts of fair Amy Robsart, pining at Cumnor Place, or of the proud woman next door?

That evening, as it was growing dark, we heard the sound of strange, unearthly music, and forthwith rushed to the window. A woman of middle age, swathed in widow's weeds from top to toe, and leading a little child dressed also in black, was moving slowly along the middle of the street, singing a wild, weird air, set to

Welsh words. Her voice was almost painfully pathetic, but her walk was quite beyond description. She would take three or four slow steps with a sort of rhythmic swing, and then stand stock still, rolling her eyes as in a fine frenzy, while she poured forth those uncanny strains with a power and pathos that made one's heart beat. Then came the swing again. The little child faithfully copied her every movement. "Is she crazy, Saint Katharine?" I asked. "Or is she a broken-down singer, on a hunt for pennies?" For her voice, cracked now and harsh in some of its tones, had been fine once. But no one paid the slightest attention to her; none of the passers-by recognized her presence even by a turn of the head. At length, slowly, still singing, she and the child passed out of sight, fading away in the gloaming.

The parish church at Conway, which is built on the site of the monastery of

Aberconway, has a fine old font and a beautiful rood-screen. The latter is said to have belonged to the abbey, but traditions differ. In the chancel are monuments to the Wynne family; and in the floor, which is lower than that of the nave, is a rude stone, with the inscription " Y. Z. 1066," — the very date of the Norman Conquest. Another bears this curious record : —

" Here lyeth ye body of Nich's Hookes of Conway Gent. who was ye 4Jst child of his father Wm. Hookes, Esq, by Alice his wife, and ye father of 27 children who dyed ye 20th day of March 1637."

Query: Did the twenty-seven children all come to an untimely end on " ye 20th day of March" ?

At length, one perfect day, we went to the castle. The old man who has the place in charge took the small fee, unlocked a door, and left us to our own devices. The whole glorious ruin was to all intents and purposes our own. During that long golden afternoon not a soul came near us, not a voice disturbed us. Could one describe a cloud, or a wave, or a sunset, so that a blind man could see it with his mind's eye? Could one give a deaf man an idea of a bird song, or the peal of an organ? As well try to do this as to describe the solemn grandeur of those time-worn, ivy-grown, moss-covered battlements, left now to the sweet winds of heaven, the flocks of rooks that fly in and out of turret and tower, and the climbing roses that brighten it with their beauty. From court to court we wandered, from tower to tower, from battlement to battlement. Here, all unroofed and open to the stars, lies the great banqueting-hall, more beautiful, more imposing, now, it may be, in its ivy-wreathed desolation, than when the gay revellers of Edward's court made its vast arches ring with song and laughter. Here still are the wide fireplaces, rich with carvings, the very ghosts of past comfort and delight. Here is the oratory, with its traceried windows and lofty, groined arches, where Eleanor the Faithful prayed. Here is her bed-chamber, communicating with that of the king, and still retaining traces of its rich ornamentation. Leading from it is an arched recess still called Queen Eleanor's Oriel, the windows of which, according to a contemporary poet, must have been finely stained: —

" In her oriel there she was,
  Closèd well with royal glass;
Filled it was with imagery,
  Every window by and by."

Here are stairways worn by feet that were stilled long centuries ago; and, in the deep thickness of the walls, the passages, dark and tortuous, through which those feet strode on errands of business, or pleasure, or intrigue. Here are stone benches that seem still to keep the impress of the forms that through the slow generations shaped and hollowed them. We looked through openings in the "crannied walls," from which death and destruction had rained on many a besieging party.

Far below us, as we stood on the lofty battlements, lay the walled town, with its massive semicircular towers, so powerful once for defence or attack, so useless now as they slept in that serenest air. Close about the castle clustered the cottages and gardens of the people, but they only added to the impressiveness of the picture. Just at our feet was a pretty stone house, its courtyard gay with flowers, the castle wall forming one of its boundaries.

It is with the beauty and grandeur of the hoary pile that we have to do; not with its history. Yet it may not be amiss to say that it was built by Hugh Lupus, first Earl of Chester, and a nephew of William the Conqueror; and was rebuilt and enlarged by Edward I., in 1284.

Descending from the heights at last, after many a lingering look at the winding river, the quiet valley, green and golden in the sun, the distant hills, and the bold headlands jutting seaward, we went down into the inner court and out on the terrace, under the windows of Queen Eleanor's Tower. Surely she must often have sat there with her knights and ladies, the fair, sweet woman whose memory is fragrant even yet, rejoicing as we did in the soft sunlight and the beauty of earth and sea.

In a sheltered nook of the inner court, an iron settee appeared a tempting resting place. Taking off our bonnets we sat there in silent thought till the long shadows fell, and the rooks came flying homeward. Then I rose and turned towards the battlements again.

Saint Katharine slowly followed. "Haven't you done climbing enough for one day?" she asked. "Where *are* you going now?"

"To pluck a rose for E. C. S. on that highest battlement," I answered. "We owe the delight of this day to him, and I must send him a rose by way of thanks."

"But here is one right at your hand," and my saint drew a pink spray from the nearest wall. "Why go any higher?"

"Because I want the very pinkest one of all, swaying against the blue sky up yonder. I'll tell you a secret too. There's been a sonnet buzzing in my brain all this blessed afternoon; and if I am ever safely delivered of it, it shall go with the rose. But — sonnets are uncertain things. — Kate! What's the matter now?"

"My purse," she said faintly, feeling in both pockets. "It's certainly gone. I've lost it. No, it isn't under the bench where we were sitting. I must have dropped it up here somewhere." — And up she flew in a successful search for filthy lucre, while I, more blessed, found the sweet wild rose that, all unknowing of its high destiny, had blossomed for my poet beyond the seas.

TO E. C. S.

WITH A ROSE FROM CONWAY CASTLE.

On hoary Conway's battlemented height,
  O poet-heart, I pluck for thee a rose!
  Through arch and court the sweet wind
    wandering goes;
Round each high tower the rooks, in airy flight,
Circle and wheel, all bathed in amber light;
  Low at my feet the winding river flows;
  Valley and town, entranced in deep repose,
War doth no more appall, nor foes affright!
Thou knowest how softly on the castle walls,
  Where mosses creep, and ivies far and free
  Fling forth their pennants to the freshening
    breeze,
Like God's own benison this sunshine falls.
  Therefore, O friend, across the sundering
    seas
  Fair Conway sends this sweet wild rose to
    thee!

At last we tore ourselves away, and the next morning took the earliest train for Caernarvon, pausing at Bangor for a view of the Menai Straits and of the two famous tubular and suspension bridges. Both are beautiful in their strength and symmetry, but the woman must know more than I of scientific engineering who undertakes to give any idea of them. Let us hasten on to Caernarvon.

The town itself was not attractive to us: solely, it may be, because it happened to be hot and dusty. It was founded by the Romans, who gave it the name of Segontium. The river that flows near the town is called the Seiont, but whether the river named the town, or the town the river, is an open question. Coed-*helen*, a wooded height opposite, tradition says was so called in honour of the Empress Helen, the mother of Constantine. In addition to its Roman history, Caernarvon was the headquarters of the English government in Wales after the conquest by Edward, — all which goes to prove that it ought to be of great interest to the antiquarian.

Leaving our luggage at the station, we sallied forth to find the castle. Travelling, like life, is a succession of choices. One cannot see, or do, or have, or be, everything. How to chose the best is the great problem. We chose the castle here. Shall I confess it was a disappointment, as oftentimes more important choices are? "More picturesque than Conway," says the guide-books, and "much finer." Externally it is in a state of almost complete preservation, and it is undeniably a grand and beautiful structure, with its well-kept walls and imposing towers. But its common-place adaptation to the uses and needs of to-day, the ground floor of the Queen's Tower being a Freemason's hall and an armoury, and the second a museum, while the lower basement of the far-famed Eagle Tower is a magazine and a drill-room, made it to our minds far less impressive than Conway, sitting silent in its proud desolation.

Yet Caernarvon, too, has its keen human interests, the associations that give it the glamour of mystery and romance. To its mighty walls, as to a fortress, Edward brought Eleanor in the spring of 1284, — before Conway had been made ready for her reception. The stronghold was but just finished, and it is said to present to-day, externally, the same appearance it presented when the beautiful and stately queen first entered the stupendous gateway which is still known as Queen Eleanor's Gate. Miss Strickland places this gate in the Eagle Tower, which is on the southwest corner, commanding the Menai Straits. But this must be a mistake, unless the local traditions and the very ground plans of the ancient castle are greatly at fault. The Queen's Gate, composed of two great towers and of Gothic arches, is at the extreme east. It is at a great elevation from the ground outside, and was approached by a drawbridge only.

At the foot of Eagle Tower we stood looking up at a small window, a mere slit in the heavy masonry. Should we venture the climb? For in a chamber lighted only by that window Eleanor gave birth to the unfortunate Edward II., the first Prince of Wales. There was but one answer to the question. Up, up, up, a flight of winding stone stairs, dark and narrow, and worn into great, uneven hollows that made the footing most insecure, we ascended, till we reached a little room, a veritable eyrie, far up in the tower. Dreary and gloomy enough it is now. It was dark, cold, and forbidding, even in the brightness of that summer day. But Eleanor was the first woman in England who used tapestry as garniture for walls, and the marks of the tenter-hooks are still visible in the small den. For it is only that, — more unhomelike than a prison cell. Let us hope that when its rough stones were well lined with soft hangings, and when perhaps warm furs and soft cushions covered the floor, it was a warm and cosey nest for the wife whom Edward was proud to say he loved "above all earthly creatures," *la chère reine* to whose memory he erected the thirteen crosses. The view from the top of Eagle Tower may well be as magnificent as the ancient chroniclers declare, but we were content with our present altitude and went no higher. "Facilis est descensus Averni"? Perhaps so. But the descent of the stairs in Eagle Tower is a thousand times worse than the going up. It is to be hoped that when Queen Eleanor had occasion to come down, there was some more royal road to *terra firma*.

Three days after his birth, — from the Queen's Gate, it is said, — Edward presented his son to the haughty Welsh barons as their future ruler, the Prince of Wales. "Give us," they had cried, "a native prince, whose tongue is neither French nor Saxon; and if his character is void of reproach, we swear that we will accept him." They were caught in a trap, yet what could they do but submit? Surely the child was a native prince, he spoke neither French nor English, and his character was unimpeachable!

It was late in the afternoon when we left the castle, and strolled slowly back towards the station. "Saint Katharine," I said, "I'm hungry. Can't we manage to get our luncheon in some place that shall have a Caernarvonish flavour? The Hotel Royal will be just like every other royal hotel. Let us do something new!"

For answer she darted into a book-store we were just passing. I followed, to find her making suit, after her own gentle fashion, to a calm-faced, gray-haired man, who was smiling benignly at her from behind the counter. "Certainly," he was saying. "Go to Mrs. Pownal's. That is the place you want"; and he pointed out the way.

Mrs. Pownal's proved to be, on the first

floor at least, a little shop, a sort of bakery, whose small counters were laden with buns, seed-cakes, tarts, and muffins ready to toast, all giving out so sweet and spicy an odour that they would have met the warm approval of Tom Brown and his Rugby friends. There should have been a school close by. "There must be," said Saint Katharine. "Think of so many tarts, and never a schoolboy to eat them!" For in all our wanderings in England we found the dame's shop-window, full of goodies, was sure to be very near the gate of the school close. This time, however, they did not seem to be in conjunction.

"Luncheon? Up-stairs, if you please," said a little white-capped maid; and up we went, through a narrow, winding way, into a cool, shaded room, with green hangings, a long, empty table, plenty of chairs, and a sofa. Its sole occupant was a gentleman, who sat before a grate in which a small fire was smouldering, notwithstanding the warmth outside. It was purely for ornament. He saluted gravely, and went on reading his newspaper.

"If you want anything foreign, you must go to the Continent," said our friends, before we started. But the whole atmosphere of that little place was foreign, even to the flavour of the gooseberry tarts. You could find nothing like it in America if you hunted from Maine to California. Why can't one put the soul of a place into words? Mrs. Pownal's was as unique, in its way, as Blossom's, in Chester. The gentleman finished his newspaper, and departed. A spotless cloth was spread for us on one end of the long oaken table, and a plentiful luncheon of cold meats, thin bread and butter, some of those fragrant tarts, and ginger ale, was served for the enormous sum of ninepence each. That, surely, was "foreign" enough for anybody. The price, I mean.

Rested and refreshed, we took the five

D

o'clock train for Llanberis, where we were to pass the night. Thus far we had seen only the fair, fertile, park-like valley of the Conway, the green heights about Bangor, and the straits of the Menai. Hardly had we left the station at Caernarvon when the whole landscape changed as by magic. Towering ranges of hills arose on either side, rough, weather-beaten, and frowning. Hedges gave place to stone walls. Over the wild and rocky pastures sheep and cattle were roving. Several times we crossed the Seiont, famous for its fishing. Near Bont Rythallt station we caught a fine view of the Eryri Mountains, with the Llanberis lakes stretching to their feet. Passing on, to the left lay the great slate quarries; to the right, the rugged hills; while directly in front of us Snowdon pierced the clouds with its mighty shaft, and the venerable ruins of Dolbadarn Castle overlooked the blue expanse of the lake. This was more like the Wales of our dreams; but before we had had time to take in the magnificent panorama we rolled into Llanberis, where a comfortable, if high-priced, hotel received us. Comfortable, if it had not been for the glaring white walls of our chambers, with the beds facing the great windows, uncurtained save by white shades, that did but intensify the glare. But we pinned up our shawls, and made the best of it, remembering Shakespeare's tourist, who says, " When I was at home I was in a better place, but travellers must be content."

We were tired enough to go to bed; but there was the pretty, picturesquely set town, at which we were fain to take a peep. Its slate quarries employ twenty-five thousand men. The owner gave them three days' holiday at the time of the Jubilee, and offered to pay the fare of all who wanted to go up to London. Only forty out of the whole small army accepted the offer. I asked why. The answer was that to the

Welsh quarrymen London seems as far off as the moon, and almost as inaccessible. No such remote and hazardous journeyings for them. The wise man stays at home of a holiday, and smokes his pipe at the door of his cabin; or he takes a stride over the hills; or, if musically inclined, he goes to an Eisteddfod.

We had been shown a photograph of a charming little inn, all gables, and bay-windows, and shaded porches, vine-covered to the chimneys, rose-wreathed, and embosomed in stately trees. It was in Bettws-y-coed, if you please, — pronounced, as nearly as I can come to it by phonetic spelling, Bettūs-y-coyd, — and it looked like a very haven of rest. There we determined to put up for repairs; and after having come to that conclusion (for we were not travelling by rule and measure), everything imaginable, from sewing on buttons and mending gloves, to the writing of interminable letters " home," was put off till we should get to Bettws-y-coed, the fair "Station-in-the-Wood." It became a standard joke, a by-word. Everything would come to pass when we got to Bettws-y-coed. Thither we went the next morning, — a sixteen-mile drive through the famous pass of Llanberis, — in a queer vehicle called a "break," not unlike a Scotch wagonette, but capable of holding at least a dozen people. A fine coach starts from another hotel, but as to this fact our landlady was, unfortunately, in the depths of ignorance. But whether by break, or by coach, the drive was something to store away in one's memory. All the way, even when we could not see it, we felt the near presence of the Welsh mountain, and knew it was towering above the long valley, with its attendant peaks, Lliwedd and Crib Coch, on either side. Much of the way the rugged hills shut us in, lifting their strong, bare, rocky shoulders close beside us, to right and to left, and leaving just space enough

for the roadway. This was as smooth and level as a floor, though we gradually ascended to the height of 1250 feet. Bordering the road, in lieu of the English hedges, were broad stone walls, so solidly put together that they looked as if they might last forever. Occasionally we caught sight, beyond, of Alps on Alps sharply defined against the clear blue sky, while the low valleys lay deep in purple shadow, or golden with the indescribable glory of that summer day.

At length we drew up before the door of the little inn of Pen-y-gwryd, "at the meeting of the three great valleys, the central heart of the mountains." As the hostlers watered the horses, we looked about us with interested eyes, for this is the scene of a powerful chapter in Kingsley's Two Years Ago; and it was from this hospitable door that Elsley Vavasour rushed, like the madman that he was, for his fearful midnight flight up the Glyder

Vawr. "P-e-n-y"—spelled Saint Katharine, looking with dismay at the array of consonants. "How are we ever to pronounce it? And how are we to remember it unless we can give it a name?"

"*We* call it 'Penny-go-rood,'" laughed the soft voice of a young English lady. "Be content with that. Of course it is not right, but you will hardly get any nearer to it." Therefore as Penny-go-rood the bright little spot, with its look of hearty good cheer, was labelled and stored away,—a picture to keep through all the coming years.

Here two Welshwomen, of perhaps the lower middle class, though it was not quite easy to place them, strode out of the inn, each with a black hand-bag, and scrambled into the two vacant seats in the break. They were incredibly ugly,—sisters, if not twins,—as alike as two peas; both tall, gaunt, hard-featured, without one trace of womanly grace or softness. Both wore plain, straight-skirted gowns of shiny black alpaca, which were well enough; but on their masses of coarse hair were perched jaunty little white straw sailor-hats, with bands and streamers of blue ribbon, forming two most incongruous halos for their harsh, middle-aged faces.

At Capel Curig we stopped for luncheon. When we reached Bettws-y-coed, the driver reined up at the door of a hotel which was not the one for which we were booked. Not for love nor money would he go an inch further. "The end of me journey, mum," he reiterated over and over, the sole response to all our entreaties and expostulations. Out came the landlady, a tall, slight, graceful young woman, who cordially begged us to alight. The pretty inn looked inviting, and she was entrancing, with her soft dark eyes and cooing voice, tender as a dove's. But we explained as well as we could that we had engaged rooms at the house of her rival, and that there our letters were to meet us, etc. Finally she magnanimously ordered her own "Boots" to drive us to the other hotel, waving us an adieu with the grace and suavity of a duchess.

The photograph had not done it justice. The low stone cottage, wide, roomy, and rambling, with its garniture of ivies and roses, now in the perfection of their bloom, in its own fair, shaded, yet flowery grounds, was prettier than any picture. The village itself is, indeed, "beautiful for situation," with the "mountains round about it, as they were round about Jerusalem." The house was full, and there was much coming and going, — coach rides and "tramps" to the hills, to the waterfalls, to castle this and castle that, and, more than all, to Snowdon. But the mending being done and the letters written, we were content to sit and rest, dreaming the hours away in pleasant idleness, two happy lotus-eaters that we were. Why should we try to see everything?

When you are in Rome, do as the Romans do: which, being interpreted, means, when you are in Wales, go to the Welsh church. When Sunday came, as the long peaceful day drew near its close, we went down the shady road and over the bridge, in search of the parish church. There is also an English church, much finer and more exclusive, we were told. But we abided by our first choice. The building itself is modern, but the grounds look so old that it is probable it occupies the site of an older structure. A pavement of broad slate flagging runs round it, bordered with shrubs and flowers. Some very old graves were in the enclosure. There were several doors, and it was a question at which we were expected to enter. Two chubby-faced boys came round the corner in great haste. "Choir boys," I said, and was fain to ask for guidance; but they vanished like two flashes of lightning. At length, by ones and by twos, the worshippers began to assemble, and we followed the crowd. It is a curious place, to American eyes, that low Welsh church, — long, narrow, with stone walls, immense stone columns, brick-paved floor in the nave and choir, and tiled floor in the chancel. Imperishable it looked, even though it is the product of our ephemeral to-day, — as if it might outlast the pyramids; and it is as severely plain as any flagstaff. The congregation, made up as it was of the common people, the working classes, interested us greatly. There was hardly a person in the seats who would have been called, in common parlance, a lady or a gentleman. The clothes worn were rough and plain, but generally clean and comfortable. Many of the men were in their shirt-sleeves. Behind us sat an old woman in black, the oddest of apparitions, who stared at us as if we belonged to another world. So small, so withered, so weather-beaten, was she, in a costume that belonged to past ages, that we certainly felt as if she did not belong to ours. A surpliced choir of men and boys — alas! that I should have to say it, but those surplices badly needed soap and water — discoursed sweet music, singing to Hamburg and other familiar old tunes their wild Welsh hymns. The air of the place was reverent. The voices in the responses were low and earnest. The young men and maidens were quiet and attentive; their elders were devout. As for the sermon, I understood but three words of it, "Apostle Paul" and "Galatia"; but it was, after all, as interesting as any I ever listened to. Earnestness is contagious, and the pale, earnest speaker held our absorbed attention from first to last. But it was easy to follow the service, which was that of the Church of England; and prayer is prayer, whether the tongue is Welsh or English.

At the close of the service a baby was presented for baptism, a tiny creature, with a long white robe and short sleeves tied with blue ribbons. The young mother was in deep black, as was the godmother. One of the surpliced choir acted as godfather, and we fancied the child's real father was dead.

With Bettws-y-coed our week in Wales ended. We wanted to go to Llangollen, sacred to the memory of the Ladies of Llangollen, and up the vale of Llanrwst, and to see the wild gorges of Carnedd, Dafydd, and Carnedd Llewelyn. But life is short, and journeyings are long. So we retraced our steps to Chester, thus gladdening our eyes with another sight of beautiful, many-towered Conway, and then slowly made our wandering way southward.

II.

BANBURY CAKES
AND THE ISLE OF WIGHT.

IT was nearly sunset when we entered the restaurant connected with the station, and seated ourselves at a little round table to await the coming of the small steamer that was to "ferry us over the ferry." For we were at Stoke's Bay, bound for the Isle of Wight.

A cool breeze swept in from the sea refreshingly. The great white room, silent and deserted at this hour, was delightfully clean and fresh, with its spotless, shining windows and dustless floor. The long counter, behind which waited two wholesome-looking women, was laden with goodies so invitingly displayed that we at once discovered we were famished.

"It will be late when we reach Ventnor,"

said Saint Katharine. "What if we were to dine here?"

We could not dine, strictly speaking; but there was plenty of delicious milk, with tarts of all sorts and sizes, and no end of buns.

"But I don't want buns," remarked one of us, removing her gloves. "I am tired of them. What do you suppose those brown things are, under that bell-glass?"

What, indeed, but Banbury cakes? "Banbury cakes, baked fresh at Banbury this very day, mem, I do assure you," said one of the attendants, smilingly.

Here was an opportunity not to be slighted. It might be the one chance of a lifetime. Had we not read of Banbury cakes more years ago than we cared to acknowledge? Had we not tasted their spicy, sugared sweetness, and inhaled their enticing odours, as we sat at Barmecide feasts with many a child-heroine in the far-away days of short jackets and ruffled aprons? And now here they were before our astonished eyes, — " baked fresh at Banbury this very day!" Banbury cakes we must have if they cost a fortune; — . and very good they proved to be, even when brought into close contrast with a child's fancy of "lucent syrups, tinct with cinnamon." Just as we finished the last crumb, we heard the whistle of the approaching steamer.

Sky and sea were both aflame as we embarked for the short half-hour's sail across the narrow channel that divides the island from the mainland, and on either low green shore cottage windows shone and sparkled in the " last red light of day." But even before we reached Ryde the gray of twilight encompassed us; and, taking the cars, we rode to Ventnor, which was our objective point, in fast-gathering darkness.

" If you go to the Isle of Wight, as of course you will," said a friend who knows

her England as she does her alphabet,
"make Ventnor your headquarters; and
if you want rest, quiet, and comfort, stop
at the 'Crab and Lobster.'"

We found all three in that quaintest of
inns, which has been in the same family
for generations, and is now at once the
pride and dependence of four young
women — sisters — who manage its affairs
and make it a home indeed for happy
wayfarers. The house itself has the advantage of belonging both to the old and
the new *régime*. It has modern conveniences combined with ancient picturesqueness. The "old house," as it is called, is
more ornamental than useful now in its
decrepitude, and is used only in emergencies. But it makes a marvellously pretty
picture with its low, broad roof, up and
over which the roses clamber, flaunting
their crimson banners from the very chimney tops, and its small latticed windows
with their snowy draperies. The whole

place was exquisite that night as we drove in behind the heavy wall of trees that shuts it from the near street in a sweet seclusion of its own. It was the height of the rose season, and every separate, dancing spray was aglow with colour and laden with perfume. Red and pink, white and yellow, the great buds and blossoms shone in the soft, bright light that streamed from every window, and from the hospitable doorway in which stood two of our hostesses waiting to bid us welcome. It was a veritable homecoming to two weary wanderers.

Here we rested in a charmed repose for three whole days. Why should we go to Cowes or to Carisbrook? Would the world come to an end if we did not see Osborne House? The curse of travelling, its *bête noire*, is the attempt to do and to see everything. It is really possible to omit some of the advertised excursions, and to leave unseen many things that are well worth seeing, and yet be none the worse for it in mind or body.

But you *must* see everything, because life is short and ways are long, and you may never come again? This is quite possible. Yet a jar, whatever be its capacity, can hold only just so much. It is better to carry home with you a few strong, clear, well-defined pictures, to be remembered and delighted in to your dying day, rather than a jumble of impressions — a medley of half-seen and wholly undigested glimpses.

So we read letters and we wrote them; we brought out our work-bags and mended our gloves and stockings; we lingered and loitered over our daintily served meals in the pleasant coffee-room where a little round table was always spread for us in front of one of the broad windows, enjoying the spotless linen, the shining silver, and the good bread, and feasting our eyes on the velvet-throated gloxinias that never failed to nod and smile at us from a great porcelain jar in the middle of the board. We pored over enticing books of travel, covering ground we had trodden, or were to tread; and we climbed the high hill against which the "Crab and Lobster" leans, ascending its terraced heights by easy, winding, flower-bordered paths, till we reached the summer-house and flagstaff at the top, from which the eye takes in the fair island and the wide sweep of the blue, far-reaching sea.

But, whatever was left out of our programme, it surely must not be Bon Church; and thither we went one sunny afternoon, through charming scenery and delightfully winding ways.

No service has been held in the little old church for more than forty years. The rusty gate was fastened, and at first it seemed as if entrance was impossible. We rattled the latch, but no one came. At last, however, as we leaned wistfully over the low paling, we saw an old man in the distance sitting on a tombstone, reading. We shouted and beckoned, and when at last we succeeded in attracting his attention, Old Mortality slowly rose and calmly surveyed us till the silver persuasion of a proffered shilling induced him to let us in. There is no eloquence to be compared with it, unless it be that of a golden guinea.

A queer, quaint atom of a place it is — this old Bon Church, built by the Saxons in the sixth century, and rebuilt by the Normans in the eleventh. If not the very smallest church in the kingdom, it must be one of the smallest. A simple parallelogram without transepts, it is so narrow that when Saint Katharine and I joined hands we could reach across the entire width of the building, our fingers coming within an inch or two of the walls on either side. The house is quite dismantled, and very little of the odour of sanctity lingers about the time-worn walls to-day, the west end being utilized as a storehouse for numberless hoes, spades, rakes, and the like. Doubtless these profane implements are used in the care of the churchyard, which is well kept and most picturesque, at once gay with flowers and sombre with yew and ivy. Here, among a host of the nameless dead, sleeps John Sterling, the friend of Maurice and Monckton Milnes, of Coleridge and Carlyle. Here lies the author of "The Shadow of the Cross," over whose low grave a long iron cross is so placed that a perfect shadow is thrown upon it whenever the sun shines.

Leaving the sleepers to their long repose, we bade good-by to our ancient, white-haired *cicerone*, and returned to our carriage. As I turned for a last look at the peaceful, sunlit spot, I caught another glimpse of him; he had gone back to his tombstone and his book.

Extremes meet. Scarcely had we lost

sight of him before we passed a thatched cottage, in front of which stood, in solitary dignity, the very smallest of wee boys. On his little curly head was a straw hat, with so wide a brim that its wearer looked for all the world like a well-grown mushroom. As we passed him, without smiling or brightening, or so much as moving a muscle of his face, he bowed down, down, till the brim of that immense hat swept the ground ; then straightening up his small figure, he stared stolidly after us, still without the least suspicion of a smile. But we laughed if he did not, wondering what impulse had swayed the small brain and led to that profound salutation.

Ventnor is famous for the softness of its air, and here are the Hospitals for Consumptives — a fine group or range of buildings, in charge of the Sisters of Saint Margaret, and under the especial patronage of the Queen. We had not the heart to visit them, as curious sightseers.

Who ever went to England without longing to hear the song of the skylark, Shelley's "sprite, or bird"? Not we, at least; yet we had not caught one clear, pure note, born of the "rapture so divine." We had been told that the Isle of Wight would surely grant us our desire. But whether we drove or walked, whether we asked the question of lady or ploughboy, the answer was always the same in effect. Oh, yes! there were plenty of skylarks. They frequented yonder meadow, or they soared from yonder hill. They sang this morning, or yesterday, or last week. If we were in a certain spot to-morrow, at a certain hour, we would be sure to hear them. But we never did. It was a good deal like John Burroughs's tantalizing search for a nightingale. Saint Katharine flattered herself that she heard the call of the cuckoo; but I was never certain even of that.

One cannot linger in Lotus-land forever, and the hour came when we were obliged to leave Ventnor. It was the morning of the Fourth of July, and surely an entirely new way of celebrating that great and glorious day had fallen to our lot. We were to go by coach to Freshwater Bay, about halfway round the island, and a distance of twenty-one miles. Not a firecracker greets our ears, not a torpedo explodes beneath our feet, not a cannon deafens us with its reverberations. But the delight, the exhilaration of that ride is something never to be forgotten.

Imagine us on the highest of the five seats on the top of the coach — so high, indeed, that we can overlook walls and hedges, and get an unobstructed view on either side. The inside of the coach, it may be remarked, is given over to the sole occupancy of hampers, baskets, and portmanteaus. How did we get up there? Let me confess that I looked and trembled, and said to my secret soul that I could never do it. But, lo! out comes the guard with a broad, strong flight of steps armed with iron hooks at the top. These are fastened to the coach, and up we walk, as easily as up a flight of stairs. Below us, in front, are two tiers of passengers, and as many more at our backs. The four horses shine like satin, and are gay with brass ornaments. Our driver, in high, pearl-coloured hat and elegantly fitting gloves, gathers up the reins; the guard, resplendent in scarlet coat and black, gold-laced hat, leaps up behind, and gives a long resounding peal of his brass horn; the porters salute; the landlady, making a picture of herself in her crisp muslin gown under the rose-wreathed porch, bows and smiles her farewell — and off we go in the clear morning air, under skies of deepest azure and by the shores of a tranquil sea. Occasionally we lose sight of the sea entirely, and wind about in what seems a most purposeless fashion, through bowery lanes; past picturesque cottages, each one of which is a rose garden to the top of its chimney; through flower-sweet nooks; through deep, dark, green recesses, cool and shadowy; beside ivy-grown walls given over to beautiful decay, and up lovely, companionable hills, verdure-crowned to the very summit.

"All we have heard of the beauty of this island falls short of the reality," cries Saint Katharine. "Can you imagine anything more perfect than this day and this drive?"

Flowers — flowers everywhere! Did they know how we loved them, the dainty darlings? They beamed upon us from every hedgerow, they gave us glad good-morrows from every meadow and roadside. As we were going up a long hill, three little girls emerged from behind a thicket, each with her apron full of wild things — common, hardy blossoms, gay and bright, and feathery fern-fronds, tied up with blades of grass. Without a word the little lassies tossed their posies up to us — a fragrant shower.

No doubt the pretty tableau was repeated day after day; and no doubt, also, that the children fully expected the shower of sixpences they received in return. But who cared? It did not spoil the picture.

A few miles further on our courtly Jehu relaxed the reins and let the horses take their own pace as we approached a stone cottage, thatched and garlanded. On the steps of the low porch stood the shyest of wee lassies in a pink frock and white pinafore, holding in her two chubby arms a shallow, tray-like basket of fresh, dewy roses, set in their own green leaves. The little creature could not have been more than five or six years old, and hardly dared to raise her eyes as she lifted her basket, shyly swaying from side to side.

There be roses and roses. Every lady on the coach exclaimed with delight over these particular ones.

"Hand up the basket, little Polly," said the driver; and forthwith the gallant, red-coated guard leaped down to receive it. Evidently "little Polly" was a favourite with the powers that be. When she darted into the house with her empty basket, every man and woman of us wore roses in buttonhole or belt, and was ready to do battle for York or Lancaster.

Whether they had flowers to sell or no, the advent of the coach was, to all appearance, a great event for the children, who made it a point of honour to wave their hats, bow, clap, and cheer as we passed by. And children abound in the Isle of Wight, as well as roses. On a wall near one small house I counted no less than eleven youngsters in battered straw hats, perched all in a row like the ten little Indians. Every hat came off, and every shrill piping voice shouted "Hooray! hooray! hooray!"

If I remember rightly, we did not talk much during that ride. Our eyes were too busy. If for a moment there was nothing else to see, there was always the ivy running rampant everywhere in riotous profusion, growing and bourgeoning out of pure delight, for the very joy of being.

"Saint Katharine," I whispered, "what do you think of trying to grow little spindling ivies in six-inch pots, and then nursing them through long Vermont winters? Yet, after all, half a loaf is better than no bread; and I know we shall go home, like other tourists, laden with 'slips.'"

Which we did; and they are alive and flourishing to this day.

Two horsemen appeared over the brow of a hill. He of the pearl-coloured hat peered forward for a moment, and then drew reins excitedly, bringing his steeds almost to a standstill as, half rising, he addressed his passengers with impressive solemnity.

"Ladies and gentlemen," he said, "yonder is the Member from Lincoln! It will be something to have seen his honour. He owns fourteen thousand acres about here — the best part of the island, in fact."

Needless to say the ladies and gentlemen, being thus adjured, were all agog to behold his honour the "Member from Lincoln." On he came, all unconsciously, a quiet old man, in a slouched hat that nearly hid his face, mounted on a brown horse as quiet and unpretentious as himself. He looked like a well-to-do New England farmer in his Sunday clothes. But oh! the magnificence, the splendour, of the groom, in high hat and brass buttons, who galloped at a little distance behind him, on a shining, coal-black charger whose dainty feet spurned the ground as he wheeled and curveted! Language fails in the attempt to do him justice. Suffice it to say that he did credit to the fourteen thousand acres and to his master's position.

Twice during the twenty-one-mile drive we stopped to change horses, during which performance home-brewed beer and glasses of milk were brought out for the refreshment of the passengers. Sooth to say, the milk was more popular than the beer, even with the men; notwithstanding the fact that a woman behind us, after disposing with great gusto of an immense mug of the foaming, odorous fluid, exclaimed as she wiped her lips, "That's the very best beer I've tasted since I drank me own brew!"

We reached Freshwater about one o'clock; whence, after luncheon, the same coach took us four miles further on, to Alum Bay and the Needles — curious rock formations with some bright colours, reminding us a little, and in a very far-off way, of the Pictured Rocks of Lake Superior. We scrambled up and down the rather uncomfortable descent, and tried to think we were well paid for our exertions; but it must be confessed the attempt was rather a failure. Then we returned to Freshwater, where we were to pass the night.

"When you are at Freshwater," it had been said to us time and again, "you will be only a mile or two from Farringford — Lord Tennyson's place."

"Yes," we answered, "and, what's more, we are going to see him."

Then would come shrugs, hesitation, and glances of dismay.

"But, my dear madam," after a dubious pause, "I — I — would hardly advise it. We seldom — that is — well, Lord Tennyson, don't you know, is not always — exactly — eh — " etc., etc.

We laughed and said nothing. It was not worth while to explain to strangers that in a sacred recess of my portfolio there was a precious letter, given me unsought — a letter that I felt sure would prove an open sesame even to the doors of that enchanted castle at Freshwater.

So, after resting and freshening up a little, we put on our best gloves and called for a carriage. As this seemed an occasion pretty well tied up with red tape, and there really was danger that we might not get near enough to the door to present our credentials, I had taken the precaution to write a little note in advance saying that not even, etc., etc., would give me courage, etc., etc., if I were not armed with the enclosed letter from our common friend X. Y. Z., etc.

"The carriage waits, mem."

Down we went. "To Lord Tennyson's," I said as we took our seats.

But James, or whatever his name was, looked at me as if he feared I was demented. Nevertheless he touched his hat gravely. "I'm sorry to say it, me lady, but there's no getting in there without a letter."

"Very well," I said. "I have one. Drive on."

We rolled along between closely trimmed hedges and past fields of deepest emerald. At length the trees to our left grew denser — a close, high wall of green.

"Lord Tennyson's park, mem," said the driver, making a wide sweep with his whip. I confess my heart beat a little more quickly than its wont. Were we really about to beard the lion in his den? But that passed, as a wave of memory swept over me, and words I had known and loved from childhood went surging through heart and brain. If a slight tremor remained, what then? There are crowned kings in whose presence it is no shame to tremble.

The house, hidden by its cordon of stately trees, was not in sight. Ere long we drew up before the lodge — a pretty stone cottage, with the usual environment of ivies and roses.

Alas! alas! Lord Tennyson and all the family, including house-servants and house-keeper, had gone, three days before, to the estate in Surrey!

And that is as near as we came to seeing the Laureate.

"But might we be allowed to drive through the park, without alighting?"

The gatekeeper was civil, and even kindly. He was "very sorry," but his orders were positive. He was not to open the gate to any one who did not bring to him a special permit from Lord Tennyson himself.

There was nothing to be said, of course. Yet our thoughts flew over the sea to a certain historic gate in Cambridge that ever swung wide at the touch of the humblest hand. We thought, too, of a library in Beacon Street, where a kindly Autocrat gives genial greetings to young and old; and of a home in Concord where high thinking went hand in hand with gentlest courtesy.

Yet still, is not a man's house his castle? Even if he be so unfortunate as to be a great poet whom the whole world honours, he is still a man and a brother, and he has a right to shut his gates upon that world if he chooses. Let us be thankful for the song, even if the lark soars so far and high amid the blue that the eye cannot follow its flight.

While we sat waiting at the lodge, a little boy and girl came trudging down through the green silence of the park to the stately gate, and tried to crawl through its bars. *He* was a sturdy, comical little figure wearing a black silk hat half as tall as himself, with a bunch of cock-feathers on one side. *She* was a wee sprite in a white sunbonnet. The gate was quite too much for him and his hat. So he gallantly pushed his little sister through the bars, then gave her the hat to hold, and scrambled through himself, never so much as stopping to brush the sacred dust from his audacious little knees ere they dashed down the road like two small whirlwinds.

Saint Katharine gave a long sigh as we turned back to Freshwater Bay.

"Just to think," she cried, "that those two babies have been playing in that park all this blessed afternoon, no doubt, and that you and I could not so much as drive through it! I wonder if they appreciate their opportunities!"

III.

A DAY OF CONTRASTS.

IT has been somewhere said that a tour in a foreign land is like reading an interesting book by glimpses and chapter headings — a word here and there, and perhaps a vivid picture, now and then, by way of illustration.

This may be. But England is not a foreign land. It is home, with just enough of a foreign element to add piquancy and flavour to the feast it offers. To one who was brought up on Walter Scott, nursed on English History, and turned loose in childhood to roam at will through the wide, enchanted fields of English literature, all is indescribably dear and familiar. To such a one, I doubt if there can be any experience on earth more utterly satisfactory than a first visit to England — Shakespeare's "precious stone set in the silver sea," — unless, indeed, a second and a third prove to be still more delightful. One is like a child lulled to rest upon its mother's bosom, listening in a half-dream as she repeats to him the dear old stories and romances that have already become part of its being, — but whose familiarity only adds to their charm. After a prolonged stay on the continent, the *homeiness* of England is perhaps what makes the strongest impression on the returning wanderer. To land at Dover, and take the late afternoon train through Kent and Surrey, when the lovely, exquisite green of the hills and valleys is all shot through with the gold of a glowing sunset, and, later on, the young moon gleams softly through a veil of silver mist, is an experience not soon to be forgotten. As for us, we were glad to see even the advertisements of Coleman's mustard, Pear's soap, and Stephen's ink.

The thirteenth of July, 1891, proved to be a day of sharp contrasts; for though geographically near each other, no two places can be farther apart in spirit than Stoke Pogis, where Thomas Gray wrote the famous "Elegy in a Country Churchyard," and Windsor Castle, the ancestral home of English sovereigns ever since William of Normandy laid its strong foundations.

Early in the morning, which means about ten o'clock in London — one being looked at askance who orders breakfast before nine — we drove to Paddington Station, *en route* for Slough, a busy little town which we reached in half an hour. But before we take the train, let a word be said about the peculiar beauty of London on just such a morning. The streets above Trafalgar Square were as yet comparatively quiet, and the roar of traffic had scarcely begun. One could not see far ahead; but as we drove on and on, the grand panorama slowly unfolded before us, the great city with its countless towers and pinnacles and mighty domes emerging from clouds of soft gray mist. Paris needs sunshine, sparkle, glitter, iridescent colour, to bring out its charm. But London — "the heart of the world," — wears her gray robes with such royal grace and dignity that one asks for no more. This, however, is only a digression for which there is no need to apologize. To digress, to turn aside from the straight road marked out by guide-books and chronicles, and find out little bypaths of one's own, is one of the greatest delights of travel. In telling the story of charmed days in dreamland, may not one take the same liberty?

At Slough we took a carriage for the two-mile drive to Stoke Pogis. For the first half-mile the way was tame and uninteresting. Then we turned into a long, straight avenue bordered by beautiful fir-trees, tall and stately, with low, wide-spreading branches that swept the ground. Not far from the church was a small stone lodge literally buried in flowers. Children were playing at the door, and a sweet-faced woman with a baby in her arms seemed the very personification of happy motherhood. The gate was unlocked, she said, and we could go in without further ceremony.

We found ourselves in a small enclosure or park, across which, at no very great distance, was the low stone wall dividing it from the churchyard proper. This we entered through an old lych-gate, a quaint, arched structure with seats, or benches, on either side. The lych-gate is seldom found now. It belongs to the past. On these narrow benches, long ago, the coffin rested, while the bearers awaited the coming of the priest.

Having passed through it we were in a broad, perfectly straight path, on each side of which grew tall standard, or tree, roses, red, white, pink, and yellow in regular order, reaching to the door of the church.

These rose-trees, all exactly of a height, with their round tops trimmed into exact symmetry, had lost all their natural wilding grace, and seemed to me the only blemish in a spot of surpassing loveliness. Their artificial splendour, for they were in full bloom, seemed out of keeping with the quiet, sylvan beauty of the scene.

On the extreme left, the yard was sheltered by a thick wall of trees that seemed to touch the sky. In the middle of what might be called a wide-spreading lawn, also at the left, rose a singular group of trees, their heads leaning together as if they might be gossiping about their rustic neighbors; and on the extreme right, close in an angle of the wall, an immense horse-chestnut stretched its branches far and wide.

Beyond this lies the churchyard proper, where " the rude forefathers of the hamlet sleep," as peacefully now as when more than a century and a half ago Thomas Gray sat beneath the shade of "yonder ivy-mantled tower" and heard "the curfew toll the knell of parting day." It is small for this over-peopled island, and not half-filled even yet. The air of Stoke Pogis must promote longevity.

The church itself is a marvel of loveliness, with its gray, ivy-clad walls, its many gables, its tall, graceful spire, and its general air of peaceful, honoured old age. Gray lies close to the western wall of the church, in the same tomb with the mother who was his idol, and in whose memory he wrote this touching inscription: —

" Here sleep the remains of
DOROTHY GRAY,
Widow, the careful, tender mother of many children, one of whom alone had the misfortune to survive her.
She died March 11, 1753,
Age 67."

I was copying this inscription, using the flat top of the tomb for a table, when the old sexton came pottering along with a basket on his arm, picking the withered roses, and trying to appear sublimely unconscious of our presence. We asked if he would let us into the church. Well, the vicar had the key; the vicarage was quite a step away; and he himself was an old man; — but if the leddies didn't mind going up into the belfry by the outside stairs, and down into the church that-a-way, they could have the privilege. Round the southwest corner we sped for a look at those stairs. They were not long, but they were very steep, and very narrow. However, there was a strong iron rail to cling to; and the outside of the church was so exceedingly quaint and picturesque that we could not afford to let trifles like that prevent us from seeing what the inside might be. So up we went, into the very queerest of dusty old places, hung with withered wreaths, crosses, harps, and all manner of funereal emblems.

They crumbled at the slightest touch, and were ghastly to the last degree as they hung there in the dim, uncertain light. Then we went down into the seven hundred year old church, to which we had come solely for Gray's sake, and found, as usual, that it was a palimpsest. Always one inscription on the parchment overlies another. The family of William Penn — *our* William Penn — were once the great folk of Stoke Pogis, and the nave of this quaintest and queerest of old churches is still hung with their escutcheons and armorial bearings. Evidently the traditions of the Penns did not all tend towards Quakerism, if Quakerism means plain-living and self-abasement. They did not enter the church by the common door, — but had their own private entrance leading through a large vestibule directly to their pew — a good-sized, carpeted room, with, I should say, at least twenty chairs in it. There they sat in state, those ancient dames and gentlemen, and said their prayers quite apart from any unpleasant contact with their humbler neighbours. On the wall is an inscription in memory of a " Son of Wm. Penn, the founder of Pennsylvania."

In one corner a square pew is pointed out, where Gray used to sit by his mother's side, thinking a boy's thoughts.

We picked some wild morning glories from the church wall, as mementos, to the dismay of our old sexton. " Why, they are only wild things, — weeds," he said, glancing scornfully at the pink and white trumpets. " I'll give you some roses." We took the roses, — but we kept the morning glories that had "blushed unseen," save for us, in Stoke Pogis churchyard. Then with many a long, lingering look behind us, we passed through a wooden turnstile and crossed a meadow-like park all starred with the little yellow trefoil or bird's-foot, to the Gray monu-

ment, of which the less is said the better.
There our carriage waited, and we soon
took the train for Windsor, only about
six minutes' ride.

It is a real relief, sometimes, to feel that
having done a thing once you need not do
it again. We were glad not to be tempted
that morning; to know in advance that, the
Queen being at Windsor, the castle was not
open to the public. The outside of Windsor Castle is a delight, something to remember, and dream of, and enjoy to the
uttermost. The inside of the majestic pile
is — to the tourist — a delusion and a snare.
Perhaps this conviction of ours is due to
the fact that it is one of the only three
places in Britain through which we were
hurried at the sword's point, as it were,
without time to think, to ponder, to recall
its past. There is no pleasure in treading
haunted ground, unless you can call up the
ghosts. As a rule, wherever we two went,
we had that pleasure. It was only at

Windsor, at Warwick, and at York, that fate was against us, and we were compelled to follow in the wake of a gaping, gabbling crowd, and to see all things as with eyes that saw not. This time we were well content to see only the majestic towers, the gray, embattled walls, the green slopes and terraced gardens, with the winding Thames at our feet, and fair Eton in the distance. These we did want to see again, and St. George's chapel, which is always open. On the way to Windsor, a gentleman in our compartment said, "Ladies, perhaps you will like to know that the Duke of Connaught is in the carriage just behind us." Then he went on to say that the German Emperor and Empress were coming in by the afternoon train.

Here was our chance! "All things come round to him who waits," I whispered to Saint Katharine. For all London had gone daft over the visit of their German Majesties. Such pushing and scrambling, such rushing and crowding, such eager attempts at seeing and being seen as had been going on around us for many days, was quite beyond our democratic comprehension, as it was outside of our whole experience. "Have you had a glimpse of their Majesties?" "Oh, you must see the Emperor!" "We are hurrying down to the Strand to see the royal procession!" etc., etc., had been dinned in our ears until we were tired.

But there were two cardinal points in our traveller's creed, one being "climb no high towers" — having grown wiser since we climbed Prince Edward's Tower at Caernarvon, three years before, — and the other, "keep out of crowds;" consequently, and in obedience to this latter clause, we had made no attempt to see the German lions. And now, here we were, by merest chance, in quiet Windsor, where there would be no crowd and no confusion; and Emperor William and his wife were coming down to say good-bye to dear grandmamma Victoria!

When the train stopped, out of the carriage behind us alighted the Duke of Connaught, shrouded in a long, dark travelling cloak. A blue cap with a broad gold band was all that distinguished him from his suite. He quickly slipped out of sight, and we stepped aside to consider the situation. A very busy and important personage was the station-master that day, — with a small army of carpenters and florists under him; but we hunted him up and asked if there was any chance for us to see the pageant of the afternoon. He shook his head. "You will have to obtain permission of his honour the Mayor," he said softly.

But either our red Baedekers, or the subtile something that always betrays an American, stood us in good stead; for when without a murmur we turned meekly away, saying that was by far too much trouble, he bade us wait a minute, and speedily disappeared. Needless to say, we waited. Presently he came back with two pink tickets, admitting the bearers to the platform to witness the arrival and departure of their German Majesties. When we offered him a fee he declined it, saying if he took it, it would cost him his place.

We went to the White Hart for our luncheon and then strolled up the hill to the castle, where we lingered until nearly four o'clock. Then we returned to the station, where the decorators had done their work bravely. From every arch, cornice, and column drooped the English, German, and Prussian colours in proud array. The royal entrance was carpeted, and banked on either side and across the platform with magnificent palms and flowering plants. Only about two hundred people were admitted behind the barriers, and we took our place among them, laughing and pluming ourselves on our good luck. For, alas! poor human nature does find a certain unholy satisfaction in doing almost without effort what its brothers have striven hard to accomplish. This may be sad, but it is undeniably true.

Pretty soon a guard of honour from the Second Battalion of the Scots Guards, resplendent in scarlet coats and enormous black fur caps, drew up in line opposite the station and were drilled and reviewed by three or four grandly appointed officers, all stars and crosses, and beribboned and bejewelled to the last degree. Next, mounted on coal-black horses with white fur saddle cloths and magnificent housings, came an escort of the Second Life Guards, in brass breastplates that glittered like burnished gold in the light of the afternoon sun, and wearing silver-gilt helmets with long white plumes. There was much prancing and caracoling and galloping up and down, until at length a mounted herald appeared, clad in cloth of gold from tip to toe. His steed wheeled and curveted, and seemed likely to throw him ; but he kept his seat bravely as he held aloft the royal ensign, and carried a shining bugle on which he presently blew a sonorous blast as the carriages from Windsor came winding down the hill.

First came several empty ones, for the Emperor and his suite ; then as many more with ladies and gentlemen in waiting on the Queen ; and then one in which sat the Duke of Connaught, wearing the uniform of the Scots Guards, and the Prince and Princess Henry of Battenberg — the latter being Victoria's youngest daughter, Beatrice.

They had but a short time to wait. The royal special train came rushing in. Every man's hat was off in a trice, but there was no noise, no shouting. The Emperor and Empress with their suites alighted, crossed the platform where an aisle was kept open for them, bowed to right and left repeatedly, got into the carriage in waiting, and were driven off. It is allowable, no doubt, for good Americans to have a little touch of curiosity as to the royalty their fathers so speedily cast off, even though, theoretically, they are supposed to regard crowns and sceptres as baubles of small account. As they passed me, so close that I could have touched them, the Emperor and Empress were talking and laughing like any common Darby and Joan, while they obviously took in all about them with quick, observant eyes. He wore the splendid uniform of one of his regiments; she, a pretty costume of heliotrope cloth, with a little bonnet to match. She is an interesting woman, attractive, without being absolutely beautiful. He has a fine, strong, thoughtful face,— a face that attracts and impresses one; and with his powerful figure and martial bearing, he looked that day the embodiment of manly health and vigor.

We took the next train for London, not caring to wait for the return pageant. But no doubt the *élite* of Windsor kept their places on that platform until the last vestige of the show was over.

"Saint Katharine," I said, as we were going to bed that night, " it was a far cry from the this-worldliness of Windsor, to the other-worldliness of Stoke Pogis."

IV.

IN THE FOREST OF ARDEN.

"The beings of the mind are not of clay;
Essentially immortal they create
And multiply in us a brighter ray
And more beloved existence."

THUS spake the creator of Childe Harold. Shall I venture to confess that when we awoke in Rugby one fine morning, with the long, bright summer day before us to be spent in wandering whithersoever our fancies led, we did not think of the town as an important railway junction, nor as the 'Rocheberrie' of Domesday Book, nor as the 'Rokebie' of Queen Elizabeth? I fear we scarcely thought even of Dr. Thomas Arnold, save as the beloved guide and friend of Tom Brown, and East, and Arthur, and "Old Brooke." We saw him with their eyes and loved him with their love.

So it was with a great flood of tenderness surging over us that, after a loitering breakfast, we made our way up High Street, at the head of which we found the famous school standing in its own green close, the embodiment of serene repose. How dear and familiar it all looked — the emerald turf, the drooping elms, the school-gates with the oriel windows above, the long line of gray buildings with the chapel at one end and the schoolhouse at the other! No flag was flying from the great round tower, for it was in the long vacation, and the whole place was as silent as "some banquet hall deserted."

As we stood looking about us, a young man approached touching his cap.

Yes. The ladies could go over the place. The houses were being cleaned and put to rights against term time. But perhaps they wouldn't mind that.

Indeed we would not, though it would have been pleasant to have heard the ring of boyish voices, and to have seen the quadrangle alive with eager-eyed laddies.

Into the Schoolhouse Hall with its great fireplaces and the two long tables running from end to end, with a third table in the corner apparently for carving and serving; into the little studies opening from shadowy passages — rooms hardly larger than closets, yet comfortable enough according to a boy's idea of comfort, and filled with all manner of boyish appliances; into the rooms of the different ranks and grades of scholastic learning — and at last into the " Sixth Form Room " — the glory of Rugby. Here were the old desks used by many a lad who afterward graved his name upon the heart of the world far more deeply than he had carved it here on bench and desk-cover. In one room — perhaps it was this of the sixth form — emblazoned on the walls were the names of those who had carried off prizes, or honours, going back, if my memory serves me, to 1834. Here in this roll of honour were the names of Arthur Stanley, and Matthew Arnold, and Arthur Hugh Clough, and many others that I do not now recall, but that were like familiar music.

"Is the Captain of the Eleven as great a man as ever?" I asked of the janitor as we stood under a great tree on the edge of the beautiful green cricket field.

"Ah, yes, indeed he is," he said. "The Captain is almost a bigger man than the Head Master himself."

"And does Sally Harrowell still roast potatoes for the boys?" Saint Katharine inquired demurely, as she stooped to pick up an acorn by way of a souvenir. "And do they buy as many cakes and tarts as they did in the days of Tom Brown?"

The young janitor — he seemed hardly more than a boy himself — looked bewildered.

"'Tom Brown?' — I don't remember the

name, my lady. Was the young gentleman a friend of your own ? He must have been here before my time ; and I don't think I know the woman you speak of. But there's a shop just round the corner where a-many sixpences go."

We had left the chapel to the last. Our guide led us to the door, but did not go in. There have been many changes and improvements since Dr. Arnold's day. The lovely chapel, with its beautiful east window, has been enlarged, but the old part is still there ; and it took but a slight effort of the imagination to see just what Tom Brown saw on that last visit of his to that hallowed spot — when he took the keys from the old verger and in the fast gathering twilight sought the burial place of his friend and master. Dr. Arnold lies just in front of the chancel rails, and near the pulpit from which he spoke such words of inspiring hope and cheer to the young, eager souls that looked up to him as to a God.

As we came out of the cool darkness and silence of the chapel into the warmth and brightness of the summer day, glad with bird-song and sweet with flower-scents, we found the janitor waiting in the porch. He touched his cap.

"Yonder are Dr. Arnold's stairs," he said; "I thought you might like to know" —and I looked with both my eyes, thinking of sundry boys in America who would remember just how Tom and East scurried up those stairs, forlorn, bedraggled, and wet, the night after their first Big-side Hare-and-Hounds.

"And over there in the playground is a tree Dr. Arnold planted," he went on. "Not in that place, though. You wouldn't think that tree was moved not so very long ago, would you now?"

It was a great tower of a tree, with wide-spreading branches, that cast deep shadows on the turf.

"When this place was repaired the tree

was in the way," he continued. "No one would hear to its being cut down. So they moved it, big as it is, and it never seemed to know it. But it cost a power o' money. Some folk put it as high as a thousand pound," — and, as he escorted us to the gate, his pride in the unlimited resources of the Rugby exchequer was something beautiful to see.

We were only eleven miles from Coventry. Was there anything there we wanted to see? Nothing but the "three tall spires" and the streets — the streets through which Godiva, that "woman of a thousand summers back," rode forth clothed on with chastity, to release her people from the grim earl's tax. Let no one suppose there is nothing else worth seeing, however. In any one of these haunted old towns one might linger for days and weeks, and not exhaust the romances written on their stony pages. I only mean that our personal interest centred in its one great legend.

One charm of all these old towns lies in the fact that no matter how many cross-roads and byways may spring up, the direction of the principal streets remains the same, year after year, century after century. We could see the whole thing — the hot summer noon, the silent and deserted streets, the white palfrey with its trappings of purple and gold, and the fair lady clothed only in the rippled ringlets of her hair. We could hear the quick beat of the palfrey's hoofs, the stir and rustle as he shot swiftly by, and the low prayer of thanksgiving and blessing from the lips of other women from whom this one brave woman was lifting a weary load. "Peeping Tom" peered at us as we passed, for alas! he is peeping yet.

We had come to Coventry by rail. There could be but one answer to the question how we should leave it. Go in prosaic, matter of fact cars from Coventry to Stratford-on-Avon? The idea was preposterous.

Ever since we entered Warwickshire the sense of awe and mystery, of an invisible presence, an intangible, quickening spirit dominating every thought and impulse, had been growing and deepening. Lichfield and Rugby and Coventry were but the doorways to the enchanted land we were about to enter. We had lingered and loitered, interesting ourselves in minor things, even as the swift swimmer, howsoever eager for the exhilaration of the plunge, the dash, the uproar of the spray, may yet linger for a moment, charmed by the beauty of the glittering sand and the curved sea-shells on the shore. How felt the knights whose quest was for the Holy Grail? Like them we were fain to put our shoes from off our feet, and veil our faces in the presence of the mystery.

We would drive through Warwickshire — the forest of Arden — the heart of England.

"You remember the oft-told story, Saint Katharine?" I said. "It is to this effect, though I don't quite remember the details.

But two men made a wager as to the most beautiful drive in all England, each asserting that the one he would name was incomparable. Each was to write his choice and the umpire was to decide between them. And lo! one wrote 'From Coventry to Stratford'—and the other 'From Stratford to Coventry.' Whatever else we miss, we can't afford to miss that drive."

What can be said about it? There is so much that cannot be put into words—the atmosphere, the glamour, the glory of it all. To begin with, it was a perfect day—as sweet and cool and bright as George Herbert's Sunday; and our hearts were in tune with the day. Fatigue dropped away from us; care was a forgotten word; even duty was a dream, hidden in some far-away nook of our New England consciences. To live was to be happy, to enjoy to the full the delight of mere existence. There were no marvels in the way of scenery; there was nothing to startle; just, for the first five miles, an almost straight road, bordered on either side by two rows of stately sycamores. But the sky was a pale blue, flecked with soft white clouds, the turf that was like emerald velvet even to the verge of the road-bed was starred with wild-flowers, the blue of the forget-me-not and speedwell, the pink of the tiny bird's eye, the yellow of buttercups, and a little unknown flower with a heart of gold. There were scarlet poppies in the fields. The hedgerows were a tangle of bloom and verdure, interlaced with ivy, and gemmed with the white trumpets of the wild morning-glory, wide open, even in mid afternoon, save where the sun was strongest. Occasionally we caught a distant glimpse of some fair mansion with a flag floating from its turret, and we passed cottages low, brown, and moss-grown, whose latticed casements were shining in the sun.

And at length there rose before us, like a vision from another world, the glorious ruins of Kenilworth — vast, spectral masses of mouldering stone, overgrown with ivy. God pity the man or woman who can stand beneath those crumbling arches, look upward to the sky from the unroofed Banqueting Hall, gaze forth from the ivy-curtained mullioned windows, or up at the mighty towers around which rooks fly, and ravens croak, without a throbbing heart and a thrill that is at once a keen joy and a sharp pain! For here one meets, face to face, the past embodied, incarnate, and yet not so far removed from us but that we can see and feel every passion that ever moved it. They who builded the pyramids belong to an age so remote that we can scarce comprehend it. Even their mummies do not stir in us any profound emotion. They are curiosities, to be studied and marvelled at in museums and wonder-galleries, not men and women of like passions with ourselves. But here we can listen for the trumpets of brave Simon de Montfort, we can clasp the gauntleted hand of old John of Gaunt, we can look into the foul dungeon of Edward the Second, we can hear the death-cry of Pierre Gaveston, who was slain hard by, we can follow the whole long procession of those who lived and loved, triumphed, suffered, and sinned, beneath the lofty battlements of Kenilworth. Elizabeth is here in all the pride of her imperious womanhood, in all the splendour of her royal state. Leicester passes in his pride of place, a lordly presence, proud, haughty, magnificent in dress and bearing, cruel in his ambition, murderous in intention if not in deed. Amy Robsart weeps in yonder tower, and glides like a spirit down those winding turret stairs that in the shadowy pleasaunce she may claim the pity of her queen. It is not what is, but what has been, that invests these ruins with such opulent splendour that imagination falters and the tongue is dumb. No magnificence of to-day can compete with the solemn grandeur of these wide, deserted spaces, these vast, silent, spectral halls, unroofed and open to all the winds of heaven.

We drove silently on to Warwick. There was no need of words.

Did I say Leicester was proud, cruel, ambitious, murderous? The next day I repented, and revoked at least one-tenth of the anathemas I had hurled at him. No man is wholly bad, even though he may be false at once to his wife and his queen; certainly not if he cared enough for his poorer brethren to found an institution like Leicester's Hospital.

One who walks up the High Street of Warwick — half the towns in England seem to have a High Street, some of which are unaccountably low — is presently confronted by a mass of stone at which he looks curiously. Is it the work of nature or of man? One sees, after a little, that it is the work of both. Through the natural rock, which has been hewn and shapen into something like proportion, a great vaulted passage has been cut; a huge gateway, through which the tide of human affairs has ebbed and flowed for ages. On the top of the mass of rock, directly over the archway, is a gray church with a square tower, so old, so weather-beaten, that it seems to be an outgrowth of the rock itself. By its side, and connected with it at an equal height, is a group of buildings equally old, equally weather-beaten. This is Leicester — or Leycester — Hospital, founded in the sixteenth century by Lord Dudley — the Leicester of Queen Elizabeth. It is not a hospital at all, in the modern sense of the word, but a home for twelve old men — twelve "Brethren." These brothers are all old soldiers, whose income from other sources does not exceed five pounds a year.

We passed through the archway and up a gently inclined plane, turned and went under a row of trees and found ourselves on a level with the church and its belongings. Just then a bell tolled softly. The brethren were assembling for morning service and we followed them reverently. It is very plain, that tiny chapel on the rock. The chancel is hardly larger than a good sized pocket-handkerchief. There is a picture — I forget what, for it had little to recommend it — over the small altar, and in the eastern window there is an old bit of stained glass supposed to represent the Earl of Leicester. But the place was scrupulously clean, the sun streamed in gloriously, throwing haloes round the bowed heads of the twelve old men, each of whom was furnished with a costly prayer-book of "fine large type," good for aged eyes. There was no music, but the broken old voices made the responses in a monotonous chant that was strangely impressive.

When we came out one of the brethren took us in charge, politely telling us he was glad it happened to be "his day" — from which we inferred that they took turns in showing the place to strangers, and pocketing the fee. Very picturesque was the bent old figure that nevertheless stepped off jauntily in its cloak, or gown, of fine blue cloth, with a silver badge — the Bear and Ragged Staff of their founder — on the left shoulder. This is the uniform, so to speak, for which the brethren have exchanged the red coat of the soldier. The badges are the very identical ones that were given by the Earl of Leicester to the original twelve, with the exception of one that was stolen and replaced in the reign of Queen Anne. Unlucky is he to whom that one happens to fall ! — for very proud are they of these ancient heirlooms. Our guide assured us that the one he wore was 350 years old, which could hardly have been literally true, as the foundation was established in 1571.

"Eighty pound a year we get, my lady," he said as he led us into the quaintly beautiful quadrangle, with its cloistered walk and balustraded staircase, "Eighty pound — which is not a bad thing," and he chuckled softly. "And we have our own apartments, and a bit of ground for a garden, and a new gown like this" — touching it proudly — "every year. And the ale is very good, very good," he added, and then called our attention to the inscriptions on the wall opposite — " Honour the King," " Fear God," "Be kindly affectioned one to another," and many similar texts, all in Old English characters. And among all the carved devices, the rich and strange architectural ornaments, appearing on every hand, in stone work, and carven oak, and fantastic timber work, the Bear and the Ragged Staff were continually repeated. Verily the Earl, whether he was good or bad, did not choose to be forgotten by his beneficiaries.

Opposite the entrance arch is the house of the Master, forming, if I remember rightly, one side of the quadrangle. A kindly man he must be, judging from the look of homely comfort that, with all its quaint stateliness, pervades the entire place.

From the garden we went to the kitchen — a spacious, lofty room with a mantelpiece of carved oak as black as ebony. So high is it that it seems lost in the dark spaces overhead. The great fireplace is fenced in, or partitioned off, by a row of high-backed settles, massive, and dark with age, arranged in a semicircle, with spaces between them through which the ruddy fire glowed. Behind these, on wall and shelf, was such an array of shining copper vessels of all shapes and sizes as it was good to see. Dinner was being made ready, and the air was full of the aroma of good cheer. The brethren bring their food here for cooking, but each has his own table in his own small parlour. After all is cleared away the hearth is swept and garnished, and the kitchen becomes a social hall, where the old men sit with their pipes and ale, a company of harmless gossips. No humble hall is theirs. If they do but lift their eyes they behold on every side the Bear and Ragged Staff, escutcheons, crests, and all manner of heraldic emblazonry. In one corner is a stately elbow-chair wherein sat James the First when feasted by the Earl of Warwick. Over the mantelpiece are crossed halberds ancient as the house itself; and on the wall is a square of needlework, a bit of faded silken embroidery, framed in Kenilworth oak. You have to look twice before you see that it represents the omnipresent bear and staff. Hardly worth noticing in its dim decay, you think; but you turn back and look at it again and again when you learn that it was wrought by the white hand of Amy Robsart,—perhaps as a love-token for her recreant lord.

We tear ourselves reluctantly away, and go on to the castle, which is not far off. Warwick is the twin-sister of Kenilworth. Their noble foundations were laid in the same year. Yet the one is a stupendous ruin, while the other is a nineteenth century home. Such is the irony of fate. But, somehow, the magnificent living castle, with all its splendid environment, with its huge, battlemented turrets, its great round towers, its long sequence of historic rooms, its stately halls and corridors, rich with buhl and ormolu, with marqueterie and bronzes, with pictures and sculpture, and ancient armour once worn by giants of an elder day — all this failed to move us as did the crumbling arches of her dead sister. Yet the picture memory gained that day was a fair one, to be kept forever. He who has seen Warwick, whether from the bridge, the court, or the gardens, can never forget its gray, dream-like, sombre magnificence.

Leicester, with many another of his race, lies in Beauchamp Chapel, in the great church of St. Mary's, with folded hands and face upturned as if in prayer. He looks as saintly as any martyred priest.

By his side is a quiet dame in hood and ruff, his last wife Cicely. Let us forgive him his sins for the sake of the one good deed that lives after him—a clear star shining through the mist of ages.

The next day we drove on to Stratford. It was like a drive in dreamland. A veil of silver mist encompassed us, softening every outline, and throwing over all it touched a bewildering grace and beauty. The sun broke forth occasionally, but only to "lower its golden buckets down into the vapoury amethyst." And soon it began to pour. We passed Charlecote, where we had intended to stop, in a sharp shower, and peered out from beneath our dripping umbrellas at its octagon towers, its gables and turrets and enormous chimney-stacks, half hidden by the overmantling ivy. We saw no deer in the storied park; but they may have been there nevertheless, for, like the countryman who could not see the city for the houses, so we could not see the park for the trees.

The storm spent the strength of its short-lived fury, and the sun shone forth again with redoubled splendour before we reached the goal of our pilgrimage, and the dream of years was fulfilled. At last we were in Stratford-on-Avon!

SHAKESPEARE.

Nay, Master, dare we speak? O mighty shade,
  Sitting enthroned where awful splendours are,
  Beyond the light of sun, or moon, or star,
How shall we breathe thy high name undismayed?
Poet, in royal majesty arrayed,
  Walking with mute gods through the realms afar —
  Seer, whose wide vision time nor death can bar,
We would but kiss thy feet, abashed, afraid!
But yet we love thee, and great love is bold.
  Love, O our master, with his heart of flame
  And eye of fire, dares even to look on thee,
For whom the ages lift their gates of gold;
  And his glad tongue shall syllable thy name
  Till time is lost in God's unsounded sea!

After awhile we went out into the quaint, old streets, intentionally avoiding that for which we came. We wandered about, now in this direction and now in that, here and there, as the fancy of the moment led; straying into this little shop where a ruddy-cheeked old woman in fluted cap and snowy apron sold plums and pears; pausing for a moment at the window of another more pretentious, with its photographs and souvenirs of Stratford; lingering, lured by a nod and smile, at some cottage door where sat a wrinkled dame with her knitting, the brown interior behind her aglow with the sunset light; returning the grave salutation of a worthy in a belted frock of white linen that fell below the knees, and with large full sleeves confined at the wrist by a broad cuff. He was old, but he was jaunty, and wore a tall, high-crowned black hat as if it had been a royal crown. He may have been a butcher, for aught I know; or his singular costume may have been that of some local brotherhood. But it was picturesque; and he might have stepped out bodily from some ancient picture-frame.

"He must be centuries old," I whispered. "Do you suppose he ever saw Shakespeare?" For it was one of the peculiarities of Stratford, as far as we two pilgrims were concerned, that we could not divest ourselves of the feeling that the whole place was enchanted, and its men and women phantoms.

We crossed the Avon, and at length found ourselves, unawares, where every landmark was as familiar as if in some previous incarnation we had seen and known it all. At our left was New Place; at our right was the Guild Chapel and Grammar School; and not far off, above its clustering trees, soared the gray spires of Holy Trinity.

Night was falling. The streets were silent and deserted. The birds were asleep, but a few lonely bats wheeled and circled round the grim, square tower of the Chapel of the Holy Guild. The air was hushed and still, with a soft, warm dampness that was full of sweet odours. And silently, as if we had been spirits, we were drawn onward until we stood at the entrance to the churchyard.

It was dark in those leafy recesses, but before the door of the church a great lamp flared, lighting the long vista of lime trees, the gray tombstones on either side, and the sombre pile above. Neither of us spoke, but slowly, reverently, and with fast-beating hearts, we passed up the wide pathway and stood hand in hand in the shadows of the portal.

For how long I know not. Then as silently as we came we retraced our steps. It is worth something, in such a place, to have by one's side a friend who understands one's mood, and knows the blessed ministry of songs without words.

The next day was Sunday, and when the bells of Trinity pealed forth we obeyed the summons. Everything seemed strange and phantasmal, in spite of the feeling of having been there a thousand times before. To stand quietly before one's mirror in the mouldy old Shakespeare Inn, arranging one's worldly, *fin-de-siècle* veil and bonnet strings, and yet to hear thrilling through the sweet, still morning air the peal of the very bells that had called to him whose memory makes every stone in Stratford a sacred shrine, saying to his soul as to ours, "Come hither, come hither!" — was not this an experience worth living for? Thanks to auspicious fate, this visit was before the new chimes of Trinity had supplanted the old.

All Stratford was going to church that morning. Earth was as bright and gay as if death and pain had never entered it. Birds sang, the river rippled on its way, the soft air just stirred the tree tops, the very gravestones were transfigured in the glad sunshine. As we passed New Place we knew we were following the very path he must have trodden three centuries ago on the self-same errand. He? Yes. What matter whether one uses a proper name or a pronoun. It is all one here. Everybody knows.

We were given seats in the choir. There was the usual service, devoutly rendered, and a sermon. I confess my thoughts were far afield, and I do not remember a word of it. But one little touch of human kindness will be always associated in my mind with the officiating clergyman that day. It so happened that there were no hymn books in our pews; and noticing this he beckoned to one of the choir boys and gave him a whispered direction. Presently the lad brought us two hymnals and hurried back to his place in time to join in the second verse.

It was Communion Sunday, and we

stayed to the holy sacrament. It chanced that as I approached the chancel rail I was, without any volition of my own, borne along towards the north end. When I knelt it was with the monument of Shakespeare above my bowed head and his sacred dust below it.

It is a comfort that some few things in this world are settled beyond all peradventure. The seven cities of Greece may quarrel as to the birthplace of Homer, but there are at least some facts in our Shakespeare's life that we know for a certainty. New Place, the home of his mature manhood, where he lived, and dreamed, and wrote, from the casements of which he must often have gazed upon the dark tower across the way, — New Place, where were the trees that he planted, and the gardens in which he delighted, and from which without doubt he was borne to his burial in yonder church, — this is not a myth, but tangible reality.

Vandalism has done its work, and but

few of its stones remain. But we know when and of whom Shakespeare bought it, and that for the last nineteen years of his life it was the place he loved best, his refuge and stronghold. One gets very near to the heart of the man in that New Place garden,—almost as near as when one stands by the grave of his brother Edmund in that grim old lady chapel of St. Saviour's.

But if this be true of New Place, what shall be said of the approach to Stratford Church? Here, too, there can be no mistake. If we are proud of our doubts, we may say it is not certain in which of the three houses owned by his father he was born. Who cares? It is enough that he *was* born. We may say that many of the relics in Henley Street are of doubtful authenticity. We may question many things in our superior wisdom, and cavil to our heart's content, if we find pleasure in cavilling. But here, on this straight pathway from street to portal, the pilgrim may feel absolutely sure he is treading in the footsteps of the Master. Here he must have walked, carrying his children for baptism; or leading little Hamnet by the hand; or leaning upon his fair Judith's strong, young arm, while he pointed out to her the birds and flowers he knew so well; or escorting Dame Anne to the church door; or giving cordial greetings to the friends and neighbours who, beyond all cavil, were proud of him and reverenced him then, even as their descendants reverence him now. Up this path, too, he was assuredly carried to his burial. The bell to which we listened this morning tolled his knell, and these skies, these fields, this river, heard the requiem.

Of course we went everywhere — to Henley Street, where the two Miss Chataways (for this was, if I mistake not, in the last year of their long reign), gave us slips of ivy from the wall; to Shottery, where

Mrs. Baker dowered us with rosemary from the old garden, with pansies, and many another common yet priceless flower.

"'That's for remembrance,' you know," she said, as she twisted the green gray spray into the posy she was arranging.

We sought the Grammar School and the hoary Chapel of the Holy Cross, where in all human probability the lad Shakespeare — son of one of the important men of the town, freeholder in his own right, owner of at least three houses, and a member of the corporation — went to school as befitted his station, and there learned at least some Greek and Latin.

But all the time it was as if we were living and moving in a dream. The present of Stratford was nothing. The past was all. The heart of the mystery, the secret of these Warwickshire fields and streams, why could we not grasp it? Why could we not fathom it? What *is* that magical, wonderful, elusive something that we call genius?

Why, of all the boys who played in the streets of Stratford town, or wandered by Avon's flowery banks, was this one William Shakespeare singled out to be not only the greatest man of his own time, but perhaps of all time ? Who shall say ?

This was my first visit to Stratford-on-Avon. Three or four years later I was at the Shakespeare Inn again. Just as before, the whole atmosphere of the place was bewildering, overpowering. I could not sleep, and, rising at midnight, I went out into the moonlit streets, in search of calmness and repose in the still, fresh air. Passing down High Street and its continuation to New Place, I leaned over the railing and gazed long at the foundations of the house under their wire screen, rebuilding it in fancy, and restoring it to its former beauty. But the grass, the roses, the trees — they were as fair, as fresh, as perfect as those that bloomed three hundred years ago. Then I turned and passed on, till I found myself again facing the old gray church with its tall spire among the stars, and the Avon at its feet. There was no lamp before the door this time; but the moon lit up the way, and the lime trees, swaying in a light wind, cast flickering shadows on the pavement. On either hand the gravestones stood as on my first visit, mute reminders of man's mortality.

I tried the door, but it was fast. Then I passed round to the south, and there I found entrance.

The moon must have gone behind a dense cloud, for not one ray of light came in through the tall windows. The place was pitchy dark. I could not see my hand before my face. But I knew I must be about on a range with the chancel, and crept along, feeling my way until I was able to grasp the rail. I can feel the cold touch of the polished brass unto this day. Keeping my hand upon it, I moved on till I reached the steps, passed them, grasped the rail again, and at last knelt where I had knelt at the sacrament, above Shakespeare's grave.

I was not frightened, I was not even greatly overawed, until I rose from my knees and found that even with my hand upon the rail I had lost my bearings — lost the points of compass. Then I said to myself, "The nave is behind you, of course. Get into a pew somehow, and sit down and wait for daylight." This I at last accomplished. I went about half-way down the nave, slipped into a pew, and rested my head upon the back of the one in front of me. Then the strangeness of it all, the weirdness, the awesome sense of invisible presences, overcame me. I could have cried out for fear, but the very fear restrained me. I dared not lift my eyes to see if the thick darkness was broken.

Suddenly a thought came to my aid. "It is true this place is full of dead folk. But they have been dead so long that it is as if they were nothing. They *are* nothing by this time. Why should you fear them?" And then I waited patiently till I could dimly discern the effigies of the Cloptons lying on their marble bed in the faint, gray light.

Then I rose, and had just groped my way to the door by which I had entered when it was opened by a withered, wrinkled old crone dressed in black from top to toe.

She carried in one hand a bucket of water, and in the other a dust-brush and some cloths.

She looked at me wonderingly, without speaking, and I made haste to explain my predicament.

"How did you get in?" she asked, severely.

"The door was not locked," I answered. "I opened it and walked in. I meant no harm."

"But how came you here? How did you know the way?"

"I had been here before," I said meekly. "I have worshipped at this altar. I knew the way hither."

"It is not possible," she said with even increased severity. "You are not old enough to have been in this place before."

Just then the great bell in the tower above our heads clashed and clanged — and I awoke to find myself three thousand miles from quiet Stratford, with the ringing of factory bells and the shriek of steam whistles in my ear. My last visit to the church of Holy Trinity was even more a dream than the first.

But who was the old woman whose precincts I had invaded? To the day of my death I shall feel that her brushes and brooms made the place sweet and tidy three hundred years ago!

V.
AT THE PEACOCK INN.

NO matter where we were, but this is what happened. "Haven't we done solid work enough for the present?" said Saint Katharine one night as we unpacked our portmanteaux, and began at once to make our rooms look cozy, comfortable, and homelike. "What if we were to turn off into the byways and hedges to-morrow? Let's go into the country, settle our brains, and hear the birds sing. Did you ever hear of the Peacock Inn?"

"Never," I answered; "where is it?"

"In Rowsley."

"And where may Rowsley be?"

"In Derbyshire. And while we are there, we may as well see Chatsworth and Haddon Hall. That is, if we get tired of the birds. What do you say?"

I said " Yes," confessing that I had had enough of mouldy crypts and dead men's bones for the present.

And thus it happened that we turned aside into beautiful Derbyshire with its rolling hills, its wooded heights, its fertile valleys.

Rowsley is one of the most charming little villages in all England; and the Peacock Inn is quaint, old, and ivy-grown, with roses blooming at the very chimney-tops, and a shield over the door bearing the date 1652. It has small-paned, latticed windows, set in deep recesses, with sills massive enough for a fortress. Surrounding it are large old-fashioned gardens that are enough to drive a flower-lover wild with envy — grounds bosky with shrubbery, where a singing brook goes wandering about under little foot-bridges; and where seats in all manner of unexpected places tempt one to careless, dreamful idleness.

Rowsley itself is a lotus-land, where it

seems always afternoon. Strolling leisurely about the lovely little village, where everybody looked well kept and comfortable, we could but wonder how the people lived. No one seemed to work save after a most desultory fashion. Up a little lane, away from everything but a wagon-maker's shop, where three stalwart men were devoting all their energies to the mending of one small cart-wheel, we found the village post-office, buried in a rose-garden and looking like a picture. Up another lane was a grocer's shop; and opposite the inn was a place where one could buy stationery and photographs. In the window of about every third house was a sign in big letters — "Tea and hot water," over which we puzzled our weak brains not a little, — discovering at last that the cabalistic words were a well-understood hint to picnickers.

We saw no signs of any other business. But the place was as clean as my lady's chamber. "Where do they put their rubbish?" I asked of my secret soul; feeling morally sure that though there was none in sight, Rowsley must have rubbish and must dispose of it. And at length I found out! That word "dispose" is well chosen. It was not thrown in unsightly heaps by the wayside, nor dumped on the banks of the beautiful river. But behind high stone walls, over which the tallest man cannot look without an effort, we discovered, at last, dumping grounds, three of them, in different quarters of that one small village. There, quite out of sight, and an offence to no one, the slow healing and assimilating process goes on by which Nature cleanses and beautifies all with which she has to do, hiding even old tin cans and broken dishes in a tangle of bloom and verdure.

But it is not for rest or birdsong, only, that one visits the Peacock Inn. Rowsley is the gate, so to speak, to Chatsworth, the stately palace of the Duke of Devonshire.

On the way thither one bright summer

morning, we stopped at Edensor churchyard, — a quiet, lovely spot where five or six of the Earls of Cavendish lie under the green turf in unpretentious graves. Edensor is called a "model village;" and nothing could be more perfect in its way. There the Derbyshire tenants of the Duke live, each in a roomy, well-built stone cottage set in a garden of its own, where all manner of flowers and vegetables run riot. The streets are carefully laid out, and the drainage and sewerage seem perfect; as for the houses themselves, they are really like a series of small villas, differing one from another, Castellated, Norman, Swiss, and Elizabethan.

Chatsworth is magnificent; a great pile of buff-colored stone against a background of wooded heights. It confronts the noonday with a magnitude and grandeur truly regal, with its gardens and stately conservatories; its terraces, lawns, and far-extending woods; its fountains leaping to the sky;

its herds of deer tossing their antlered heads under grand old trees, and its picturesque stone bridges spanning the clear waters of the Derwent. We went through the house, of course, — which is like other show places : a bewildering labyrinth of halls, courts, drawing-rooms and galleries, of pictures and statues and bric-a-brac, which we scarcely looked at, and made no effort to remember. Show places, however magnificent, had small attraction for either of us; and we were glad to make short work of this one. The family were not in residence, and I asked one of the servants if the Duke came often to Chatsworth. "Oh yes, mem," he answered, " he comes always in the back part of the year—about Christmas time ! "

And, sure enough, he came the next December, as usual, — the seventh Duke of Devonshire, — an old man of eighty-three, — to sleep with his fathers and his sons in Edensor churchyard. His later years had been full of sorrow and bereavement. One who knew him well says: "Pathetic indeed in later years was the figure of the Duke as he sat at the head of the long table in the great dining-room at Chatsworth. His grave, strong face, the crown of white hair which fell carelessly over the high, broad forehead, the eyes alive and alert with a fire that seemed still young, the dignity, the beautiful, quiet distinction of manner, the stamp of intellect on the features, the bearing which had all the courtesy of an earlier century and was not the less stately for the bent head and the slight stoop — all these traits gave to him the air of one of the portraits by Titian or Van Dyck that hung hard by. His simplicity was that of the grand seigneur, and so was his genuineness; never in his life had he felt called upon to seem something he was not."

There are landlords and landlords. This man's management of his vast estates commanded the unwilling admiration of his political opponents, and extorted approval even from the Land League.

After leaving the Hall we wandered off by ourselves through the stately green solitudes in search of the real object of our visit, a stone tower surrounded by a moat still filled with sluggish water. It is called Queen Mary's Bower. Chatsworth (an earlier building, however) was one of the prison-homes of Mary, Queen of Scots, during her eighteen years' captivity. There, as the polite phrase is, she was "placed in the charge" of the famous Bess of Hardwick, Countess of Shrewsbury. When allowed to wander out of doors, this tower was her favourite resort. Over the broad stone stairs that still lead like a bridge upward across the moat, her slow, desponding feet must have passed many a time, that she might reach a little square enclosure on the other side of the tower.

It is hardly more than ten feet square,

a mere pocket-handkerchief, as it were. But here with her own hands she planted and tended a little garden. The rich green turf of England has crept over it now, obliterating every trace of shrub and flower. We could not find within its narrow walls even one daisy to press. But the silent spot moved us strangely. It was our last thought as we left Chatsworth.

Should we attempt the walk to Haddon Hall, or should we not? The directions given us were most enticing — a bewildering tangle of green lanes, old stone gateways, cottages, footpaths, beech plantations, wooded heights, sloping pastures, little pools, quaint turnstiles, and broad green drives. It was a great temptation; but we did not yield, strong-minded women that we were. On the contrary we went home to luncheon, leaving Haddon for another day.

Haddon Hall is an ideal specimen of an old baronial mansion, still in a fair state of preservation, although it has not been used as a family residence for two hundred years.

The approach to the Hall, which is on high ground, rising steeply from the banks of the river Wye, is incomparably beautiful. Haddon is as redolent of medieval state as Chatsworth is of modern splendour; and it is all alive with poetry and romance. The custodian lives in a pretty lodge at the foot of the hill, in the garden of which yew-trees are clipped into the rude semblance of peacocks and boarsheads, the crests of the Manners and Vernons. His three young daughters were knitting on the steps leading to the great entrance hall, and gave us smiling welcome.

We were the only tourists abroad that morning. Haddon Hall is just a little off the common route of tourist travel. In other words, it is not one of the stock places whose very name is a shibboleth that every American traveller feels bound to pronounce or die in the attempt. For this reason, or because of the good luck that seldom failed us, we had the beautiful old place all to ourselves that summer day. Surely the very stars in their courses must have worked for us — for in four months of happy loitering in the highways and byways of England, we found ourselves but three times at the heels of a gaping crowd. Ah, the difference!

The lassies gladly led us from room to room, letting us linger and loiter at our will. To fully understand the charm of the place, one needs to know that the estate of Haddon was given by William the Conqueror, not long after the battle of Hastings, to his illegitimate son, William Peveril, a descendant of whom is said to be Walter Scott's "Peveril of the Peak." The Peak is Haddon; or perhaps it is wiser to say Haddon claims to be the Peak. Those were troublous times, and the place passed in the reign of Henry II. into the possession of the Avenels, and thence by marriage to Richard Vernon.

History repeats itself continually, and so does the "old, old story." Derbyshire had its Montagues and Capulets, its Romeo and Juliet. The Vernons who owned Haddon Hall, and the Manners, the family of the Duke of Rutland, were at sword's points. Almost as a matter of course Sir John Manners fell deeply in love with the fair Dorothy Vernon, the daughter of Sir George Vernon, called the King of the Peak, and the last of his name that lived at Haddon. The natural consequences ensued. Tradition says that Sir John disguised himself as a forester, and haunted the Haddon woods, thus obtaining brief glimpses of his lady love, and now and then a stolen interview with her. Tradition farther saith that on the night of her sister's wedding she stole away from the gay company in her gala dress, fled down a flight of stone steps, still known as "Dorothy's stairs," glided, a fair, white, trembling vision, through the long length of the shadowy terrace, and crossed a quaint foot-bridge where her lover awaited her. Away they rode into Leicestershire, where they were married the next morning.

But this escapade ended the feud. The two papas forgave the adventurous young couple, and on the death of Sir George, the estate of Haddon Hall passed into the possession of Sir John Manners and his beautiful Dorothy. The Manners and Vernon arms are quartered together on a shield over the door now, with the legend, "God save the Vernons," — a worthy tribute from a former foe.

If one could only put impressions into words, and convey to other senses the perfume of the flower! Lingeringly, loiteringly, we roamed through the great mansion. One of the young girls with her knitting-work was ever within call, ready to answer questions, if questions were asked, or to be silent when silence was golden. Everywhere there was a hushed repose, a tantalizing reticence — as if the very walls could have spoken, but would not. One listened involuntarily for footsteps and whispers.

We went from the chaplain's room — so-called — which seemed anything but sacerdotal, with a pair of ancient jack boots and a leathern doublet in lieu of priestly vestments — to the curious old chapel, rough, massive, almost rude, in spite of some fine Norman work and a stained-glass window of the fifteenth century; from the huge kitchen, with its enormous blackened fireplace, to the panelled dining-room. Here is an oriel window overlooking the garden, where many a fair dame, no doubt, sat with her maidens round her in the springtime of the year. Then on we passed through the great banqueting hall, an apartment worthy of its imposing name, with its raised dais, its minstrel's gallery, and its long oaken tables that once groaned beneath the weight of boar's head and wassail bowl, into the drawing-room hung with old tapestries, marvellous to behold, and rich with carvings and panellings, black as ebony. Here, too, is a great fireplace, with curious, half-alive, self-asserting andirons, reminding one irresistibly of those Iachimo took note of in the bed-chamber of Imogen. Hard by was another bed-chamber, that of the Earl ; and here, as if to emphasize the truth that it is but a step from the cradle to the grave, we were shown the hooded nest in which Sir George Manners was rocked when a baby, and the canopied bed in which he died. Tapestries, dim and faded in colour, but wonderfully preserved, adorn the walls, and reaching from the mantelpiece to the ceiling were stone carvings, grotesques of every imaginable shape — that looked as if they might have been born of the pyramids.

Of course we saw the bed where Queen Elizabeth once slept " in maiden meditation fancy free." The stately vestal must have been something of a gad-about. She seems to have slept in full one-half of the state chambers in England, — as Charles I. did in the other half. We paced the long ball-room — so long that the receding vista dwindles almost to a point, and magnificent with carved oak and floriated ceiling — and at length descended to the garden by the very stairs down which Dorothy fled, and found ourselves on the terrace with its balustrade of arched and battlemented stone, and its enormous, wide-spreading yew-trees.

But days, even summer days, are short, and travellers' ways are long. We could not stay at the Peacock Inn forever. On our last Sunday we attended service in the village church, about two minutes' walk from our abiding-place. In a small chantry, shut off from the nave by crimson curtains, is a recumbent figure in white marble, — that of the young wife of the present Duke of Rutland. A little child lies by its side, and a lily has just fallen from the nerveless hand.

In the afternoon it rained, and the guests of the house petitioned for a fire in the coffee-room. Presently it was blazing away on the old hearthstone; and another lighted up the quaint, brown-raftered hall, with its carved oak furniture, black with age, and its curious relics of bygone days. Among these is a funereal tablet, telling of the death of a certain Duchess of Rutland in 1700. It has hung there ever since, and records not only her transcendent virtues, but the fact that she "died of a stricture," whatever that may be.

We gathered about the two fires, strangers from many lands, and I see that my note-book declares that it was "very pleasant," — a statement that certainly does not lie open to the charge of womanish exaggeration.

VI.
AT HAWORTH.

WE had come up from Lincoln *via* Dorcaster and Bradford into the very heart of the West Riding. "Next station is Keithley, ladies," said the small boy who punched our tickets. "Change there for Haworth."

"Keithley?" Our maps and guide-books were silent as to any station of that name; but a moment's consideration only was enough to show us that "Keithley" was the local pronunciation of Keighley, a place well known to all lovers of Charlotte Brontë, and known, doubtless, to others as well. Yet I fancy few Americans ever gave a thought to the busy manufacturing town save in its connection with the three gifted women to whom, comparatively insignificant as it is, it was the door that opened into the wide, unknown world beyond it.

Into the station we rolled at last, and found we had an hour to wait for the train on the branch road to Haworth.

"Meanwhile, shall we explore the town, Saint Katharine?" I asked.

But she answered in unsaintly wise: "We have been exploring too many cathedral crypts, wherein are dead men's bones — and other things. Let us save what little strength is left us for Haworth."

So to the waiting-room we went, where a calm-faced, black-gowned woman sat at a little table, sewing. She rose, smiling, to do the honours; and at once the atmosphere of the place grew kindly and homelike. Courteous and attentive before, she grew heartily cordial as soon as she found we were going on a pious pilgrimage to Haworth.

"Many people went there in the old days; not so many go now," she said.

"But how is that?" I asked. "Surely, it is not yet time for the Brontës to be forgotten!"

"Indeed it is not that," she replied, "though many folk have short memories. But since the parsonage door has been shut in the face of all who come for the sake of them who are dead and gone, and since the new church took the place of the old one, it's only now and then that a stranger cares to go to Haworth,—or those who are not strangers, either," she added after a little.

"Then we cannot see the parsonage?"

"Ye can see the outside of it. None can hinder that. But it's no good trying to get in. I'd advise ye not. He's a bit comical, the parson is. Yes, we call him a comical stick. He's like the ortz," which, as near as we could make out, was some wayside plant, with a gnarled and crooked stalk. Never having heard of it before, however, the full force of the simile was quite lost upon us.

The station woman was well read, at least in "Shirley," every detail of which she had at her tongue's end.

"You should go to Liversedge," she advised. "That was the scene of 'Shirley.' There's many a one can show you where were the hall and the old mill and the rectory. And they do say that Shirley were Miss Emily Brontë herself."

We looked for bleakness and barrenness as we approached the region of the moors. Instead of this, the country had been growing fresher, greener, and more picturesquely beautiful ever since we left Bradford; and the rolling hills made our hearts bound after the low, flat lands of the "fen country" and Lincolnshire. When the train stopped at Haworth, and we stepped out upon the uncovered platform, we could not believe our eyes. Haworth? Was this Haworth, — the Haworth of Charlotte Brontë? Impossible! Before us, in the narrow valley through which the railway ran, lay a spick and span new village, with tall, smoking factory chimneys dominating over the long rows of tenement-houses, — houses which were gradually creeping up the higher ground beyond. But where were the church and the parsonage and the Black Bull Inn?

The guard hurriedly deposited our luggage upon the platform, and the train swept on. Not a porter was in sight, not a cab, nor a "four-wheeler." But, presently, a young fellow, wearing a gold-banded cap, came to our deliverance. Haworth, old Haworth, that is, was on the other side of the station, quite out of reach of our present point of vision. Forthwith, he piloted us across; and towering above us, "so near and yet so far," was the goal of our desires.

But how were we to get there? Up the steep height that seemed almost perpendicular climbed a narrow lane bordered on each side by a low stone wall. Our new friend eyed us from under his visor. "It's not so very far," he said, "but it's steep. Ye can walk, and I'll carry the luggage."

"But where are your carriages?" I cried in dismay. "Are there none here?"

He shook his head. "Well, they doesn't often coom to the train," he drawled dubiously. "Ye'd have a long wait, and it 'ud cost ye all o' two an' sax, an' mebbe three shillings."

Evidently, such reckless extravagance was not countenanced in Haworth. We bade him gather up our belongings and lead the way. Two portmanteaus, two handbags, and a shawl-strap. He wrestled with the five pieces for a while in a vain attempt to handle them all, then regretfully called a small boy to his aid, and the procession started.

It was very much like trying to walk up the side of a house, provided the house had an uneven surface, and was well set with cobble-stones. At length I stopped for breath. Still far above us loomed the gray church tower, and I knew the Black Bull Inn was next door to it. "It'll be easier after a bit," said our guide, consolingly. "But them as built this town in the first place built it the wrong way altogether. I never could see the reason o' it."

Saint Katharine and I sat down on a conveniently broad stone in the low wall, to laugh as well as to rest, and our escort followed our example as he wiped his flushed face.

"Did you know the Brontés?" I asked as we sat there.

"No. They were all dead afore my time. I wor not born here. I'm from Derbyshire. But I wor thinking it wor for them yo coom."

"You are right," I answered. "But we are told that we cannot see the parsonage. How is that? Do you know?"

"I knows little about that," he said with some hesitation. "But I knows *him* very well. I sings in the choir." And he blushed under his tan, as he beamed all over. Evidently, it was a great thing to sing in the choir.

Up we went, higher and higher. The new town lay at our feet: the old one was still above us, with the moors stretching far beyond.

We began to have a fellow-feeling for the Haworth doctor, made famous by Mrs. Gaskell, for whom, when he refused to come to the aid of the lad who was bleeding to death, this apology was made, " He's owd, yo seen, and asthmetic ; and it's up hill."

But at length we turned into a sort of paved court, or winding way, broader than the lane, and came out at a right angle upon a street paved with rough flags and cobble-stones, and hardly wider than a wide garden path. I had completely lost the points of compass, but I fancied it was east and west. It was as steep as the ascent we had made in the other direction, and was built up as closely as a city block, the queer, irregular houses of varying heights, but mostly tall for the width, or rather for the narrowness of the street, looking as if they had been pressed together, and had thus crowded each other out of shape. A heavily loaded cart was toiling up the hill, drawn by four clumsy-footed horses, with high, oddly shaped collars, all harnessed tandem. And for a good reason. There was not space enough to drive them abreast.

"This is what we call the main street," our guide announced proudly, with an inclusive wave of the hand.

We looked up and down: at our left, the long, narrow, steep descent; at our right, and but a little way off, the street made a sharp curve, and ended in a small, irregular plateau, which is probably in English fashion called the market-place. Just at this curve stood the Black Bull Inn, in the very shadow of the church. To say that our hearts sank within us, so dark, so grim, so altogether forbidding, did the old hostelry look, is to use a very tame expression. But it was the best in the place; and who would have gone elsewhere, even if it had not been? So, after paying our young choir-singer two shillings, which he had certainly earned, and congratulating ourselves on having saved all of one shilling by walking, we proceeded to investigate. Entering the door, which was on a line with the street, we found a hall or passageway, with low, dark ceilings, and a stone floor full of inequalities, out of which, round a corner, rose a flight of stone stairs, worn into such great hollows by the tread of generations dead and gone as to be positively dangerous. In this hall hung, by actual count, fifteen hams in the process of curing. On the left, however, was a little coffee-room, comfortable enough, with its smart carpet and hair-cloth sofa, into which we were escorted by the landlady herself.

Could she give us a room with two beds? For we two lone women felt a strange unwillingness to be separated that night.

No, she could not.

Could she give us two adjoining rooms? No, she could not.

What, then, could she do?

She could give us one room, with one bed, but not two rooms. For if any commercial traveller should happen along, it would be "awkward" (her own expression). How could we expect the luxury of a room, or even a bed, each, when there were but two guest-chambers?

But we could take our choice of the two, that was one comfort. So up we went, picking our way carefully, and expecting to find the accommodations offered of most primitive fashion.

We had already learned to look for incongruities. But our surprise thereat was seldom greater than when we found in those little, low-ceiled chambers perhaps the richest and handsomest old mahogany furniture we had seen in the United Kingdom, with linen and appointments to match. Bedsteads and bureaus, massive and finely wrought, were dark as port wine and shone like glass.

We made our choice; and forthwith the landlady deprecated it, and strongly advised us to take the other room, giving as her chief argument not only that it was the finer, but that most visitors preferred it, because it overlooked the graveyard! We abided by our first choice.

Could we have a carriage to take us at once to the moors? The afternoon was on the wane, and already the sunset was beginning to kindle its fires in the west. How far was it to the waterfall, — Charlotte Brontë's waterfall? It was a matter of several miles. If we were to see it, we must ride, much as we would have preferred to walk. But there was no carriage; and, if there were, there was no man about the premises but the hostler. And he wasn't there, either, having "gone somewhere" that afternoon. It was only after prolonged discussion that we succeeded in making our hostess understand that the excursion could not be indefinitely postponed, and that, if there was anything to ride in in Haworth, we wanted it immediately. She meditated placidly. Could we go in a dog-cart, for instance?

Yes: we could go in a dog-cart, a donkey-cart, a hay-cart, or any kind of a cart.

It appeared at last, that dog-cart. I climbed up beside the driver, Saint Katharine got in behind, and off we started. It was worth all the trouble, and something never to be forgotten, that drive in the flush of the golden sunset, up the breezy hills and over the moors stretching far and wide like prairies, and just beginning to take on the purple glory of the blossoming heather. Our driver was a Haworth man, born and bred; and very well did he know the story of the sisters three who had made this out-of-the-way Yorkshire village a Mecca. He, too, knew "it was for them ye coom."

On the top of a hill from which it seemed as if the lonely moors stretched on every side to the horizon, he brought his swift-footed black pony to a standstill. We were but a few minutes' walk from the little waterfall which was a favourite resort of Miss Brontë's, and by the side of which, tradition says, she wrote many chapters of "Jane Eyre." Thither we went.

The water was very low, for a long drought had dried up half the springs in England. A slender stream trickled sleepily over the stones, and that was all. But the little green dell was quiet and secluded in the midst of the brown and purple of the moors, the air was sweet and fresh, the sky overhead was both blue as a sapphire and pink as an apple-blossom; and it was good to be there. Nevertheless, I had serious doubts as to those chapters of "Jane Eyre." Writing under shady trees, to the tune of a tinkling waterfall, is all very well in theory, but it is apt to be quite another thing in practice. The poet betakes himself to the sunny pastures or the woods, and vainly essays a song in praise of the golden afternoon. Both voice and harp are out of tune. The next morning, in the dulness of his study, maybe with the autumn rain dashing drearily against the window-panes, the song sings itself.

As one sees the moors from a carriage it seems impossible that an adult in his senses could lose his way. The stories of such mishaps seem fabulous. But, when we were out of sight of the highway and the dog-cart and attempted to retrace our steps, we found it not quite easy to say whether we had come this way or that way. To an unaccustomed eye, while there are many paths, there are few landmarks; and we could see how one might wander up and down and roundabout, and be long in finding one's way out. As we climbed to our seats again, we said as much to our driver.

"Yet," he said, "there's many a one about here who can set snares for the grouse of wire no thicker than a hair, and with nought to mark the place, and go and lay his hand on them wi' his eyes shut."

"But how?" we asked. "How can he find them?"

He laughed, shrugging his shoulders. "That's what they don't tell," he said; and, not caring to pry too closely into the secrets of the poachers, we were silent. Presently he stopped again, and pointed with his whip.

"Ha' ye read Mrs. Gaskell's book?" he asked. No need to ask *which* book.

"Yes," we answered.

"An' do ye mind the story o' the old woman an' her calf? How she met Miss

Brontë one day walking hereabouts, an' cried out to her, ' Ho, ho, Miss Brontë, ha' yo seen anything o' my cofe ? ' Miss Brontë said how could *she* tell, for she didn't know the calf. ' Well, nah,' said the old woman, ' it's a-getting up nah betwixt a cah an' a cofe, what we call a stirk. Will yo turn it this way if yo happen to see't? Ah, do now, Miss Brontë.' Do ye mind the story ? "

Yes, we remembered it. Could anything show more clearly the simplicity of her relations with her father's flock ? He went on : " Well, then, do ye see the little house yon, under the last clump o' trees ? That's where ta old woman lived."

It is my impression he said *lives*. But, as the incident he referred to must have occurred at least thirty years ago, it is best to be on the safe side, and not assume the rôle of a resurrectionist.

We returned to the inn, with our hands full of heather, and, while supper was being made ready, went out for our first near view of the church and parsonage. The former has been not so much restored as pulled down and built over again. Nothing is left of the church of the Brontë days but the tower. We made no attempt to go in that night, neither did we wander long among the graves. Anything drearier, darker, denser, and more uncanny, than that old graveyard, where the dead seem to lie huddled one upon another, tomb hustling tomb in the deep shadows of tree and church tower, it would be hard to imagine. Perhaps the hour had something to do with it, and the low soughing of the wind. But we were glad to pick our way out as rapidly as we could, treading upon grave mounds in spite of our care, and feeling as if we were crushing hearts beneath our feet.

Once out, however, upon the footpath that runs along the wall of the churchyard to the parsonage, we found the earth was still bright with the lingering afterglow of sunset, and took courage to go on. There is no need to tell here how the Haworth parsonage is situated. All the reading world knows how it faces upon the churchyard, which, indeed, surrounds it on three sides. A narrow yard lies between it and the place of graves; and from the lower windows of the house the tombstones may possibly be hidden now by a belt of trees and shrubs that look as if of recent growth. The tiny court was gay with scarlet geraniums and other bright-hued flowers that night; and as we looked longingly through the paling that divides it from the by-street, or lane, (at the end of the house) we saw two young lassies trundling hoops, and heard the sound of merry voices. Doubtless the house as well as the church has been "freshened up." But it is the same unpretentious gray stone house, nevertheless, with the same walls and the same windows; and we knew well in which one of those front chambers the short, sad life of Charlotte Brontë went out.

After supper we sat long in the gloaming, looking out upon the little market-place from which three or four steep, narrow lanes struggled hither and thither. It was a strange picture, as foreign in character as if it had been in the heart of France instead of England. Across the way was a small shop, where somebody advertised himself as " Dealer in Wines and Liquors." On a wooden bench by the side of the door, four men, one in a blue blouse, and one with an imposing gray beard and skullcap, sat indolently lounging as they smoked their long clay pipes and discussed Yorkshire politics with many gestures and loud vociferation. To them presently appeared a Salvation Army woman, in quaintly fashioned black gown and poke-bonnet tied down with a red ribbon, with a bundle of tracts under her arm, which

she proceeded to distribute, or tried to.
There was much good-humoured jesting
and coarse laughter, in which she joined
as heartily as they; but not a man took
one of the little pamphlets. Soon another
"hallelujah lassie" from the barracks below the village joined her; and they went
on their way, bandying jokes the while
with the men they left behind them.

Yet I heard afterwards that the Salvation
Army had done great good in Haworth.
Far be it from me to gainsay it.

Diagonally across from our window, on
a long flight of stone steps leading up to
what we took to be a school-house, half a
dozen children in wooden shoes, some of
them mere babies, were playing, to the
imminent peril of their necks, their heels
making a tremendous clatter as they raced
up and down. Still farther on were more
steps; and on the corner of the building
to which they led was the sign "Post-
office." England is not a land of rapid

changes. We wondered if that was the very spot from which "Jane Eyre" went to seek publisher after publisher, and to which, after weary waiting, flew the flocks of white-winged messengers that bore to the shy and sensitive woman the story of recognition and renown.

"Saint Katharine," I said, "we will settle that point to-morrow."

And we did. It was the identical place, — a humble little shop, with one corner set apart for the public service. What stories its walls could have told if they had had but tongues!

But this is a digression. While we were still at the window, a young and handsome cavalier came clattering up the street, rode straight up to the inn door, nothing daunted by the spotless, broad stone flagging, and without alighting knocked imperiously with his whip. Out came the bar-maid, stalwart, red-cheeked, and round-armed, with a pitcher of foaming beer and a mug which he held while she filled it with the frothy amber. He sipped it slowly, smiling and talking the while, as he smoothed his horse's "chestnut mane," then dropped his sixpence into her outstretched hand, and galloped away in the deepening twilight. Was he one of Robin Hood's men, reappearing in this matter-of-fact century? For Robin Hood, a real man and no myth, lived near Liversedge; and his grave is still shown to the curious.

When we went to our chamber, Saint Katharine eyed the high bedstead inquiringly. "The question that disturbs my mind just at present is this," she said; "how are you ever to get up there?"

"Behold, O thou of little faith!" I cried, drawing the drapery aside, and displaying a flight of carpeted steps, up which I soon mounted triumphantly, to be lost in the abysses of a huge feather bed.

We were not long in learning why our landlady had so strongly advised us to take the room "overlooking the churchyard." Dead men tell no tales; but the men of the village, who, one by one, dropped into the room beneath us for their pipes and beer, and perhaps a drop of something stronger, told many; and a merry racket they kept up till midnight. All night we heard the church clock strike the quarter-hours, and thought of other ears that had listened to it wearily in the long night watches. And at early dawn the clack, clack, clack, of the wooden shoes began again.

Need it be said that we thought, too, of the gifted and misguided Branwell Brontë, who had sown the seeds of all his misfortunes in that very inn? At breakfast, the maid who waited kindly hoped the ladies had not been disturbed by the noise. Then, as if by way of apology for the carousal, she added, with some hesitation, "It was here, they say, that Bramwell, as they call him, used to come."

Poor, brilliant, ambitious, unfortunate

boy, — his very name mispronounced under the roof to which he had been so often summoned, that his wit and precocious cleverness might add sparkle and fragrance to the wine! In what seemed to be a sort of state apartment, back of the one under ours, we were shown an odd, three-cornered chair, in which he was wont to sit enthroned as king of the revels.

After breakfast we sallied forth on a voyage of discovery. Just below the sharp curve in the street we had noticed a small stationer's shop, in the window of which was the familiar photograph of Charlotte Brontë; and thither we went.

"Robinson Brown" was the name over the door. Might he not be kith or kin to that very Martha Brown who was for so many years poor old Tabby's faithful assistant, and who, Miss Brontë herself bearing witness, "waited very nicely" when the Bishop of Ripon made his memorable visit to the Haworth parsonage?

Behind the counter we found an exceedingly pretty young girl, with an abundance of wavy, reddish hair, an exquisite complexion, and laughing blue eyes. Yes, Robinson Brown was her brother; and Martha Brown, who died only two or three years ago, was their aunt. Their father, who was dead also, had been sexton of the church for forty years, during the whole incumbency of Mr. Brontë.

Was her mother living? and would it be an intrusion if we went to see her? Yes and no. Her mother loved to talk of the old days, and she had some relics of Miss Charlotte that she would be glad to show us.

Not far from the Black Bull Inn, one of the narrow lanes makes a swift descent. Half-way down it, we came to a little, low house, quite on a level with the street. Not even a door-step intervened. Over the door an inscription was rudely hewn in the stone casing, after this fashion : —

"I. S.——A. S.
1 6 7 1,"

which, being interpreted, means, "Is as it was in 1671." Lifting the black knocker, we were soon admitted, and led through a small passageway, carpeted with oil-cloth, into a large and comfortable room, as neat as wax, the stone floor being scoured to the last degree of whiteness. It was evidently the kitchen and living-room. But there were in it two or three pieces of handsome old furniture, dark, lustrous, and brass-handled. There were some pictures on the wall, and a bird-cage in the white-curtained window. A young woman was ironing at a table under the window; and at another in the centre of the room sat Mrs. Brown, the sexton's widow, on some housewifely task intent. She was a pleasant-faced, elderly woman in a black cap. The merest hint of our reason for seeking her insured us a most cordial welcome.

"Charlotte," she said to the ironing maiden, "go fetch the little cradle."

"Is your daughter named for Miss Brontë?" I asked, as the girl disappeared.

"Yes," she answered, with but very little trace of the peculiar Yorkshire dialect, her daughters having none of it. "She wor born just a month after Miss Charlotte died. She wor very fond of my children, Miss Charlotte wor; and, when my babies wor a month old, she would always ha' them brought up to the house. Miss Charlotte wor *good*. So wor they all, always thinking of poor folk, and trying to help them."

Here her daughter returned, bringing the "cradle" and a small box. The former was a mere toy, — a little wooden cradle, from which the head was broken, in which the child Charlotte had rocked her dollies, crooning soft lullabies, no doubt. I held it in my hand reverently. No fragment washed ashore from the sea of her later literary life, no relic of her womanhood, could have brought her so vividly near. And was it not a comfort to know, by ocular and tangible demonstration, that the lonely, motherless little creatures in that silent parsonage had had dolls, and had cuddled and fondled them like other children?

The box contained a few odds and ends, — ribbons and bits of lace that Charlotte had worn, with a bow from her last bonnet, — all sacredly treasured by Martha Brown and bequeathed by her to her niece.

The story of the Brontës, as we heard it that day from the lips of Mrs. Brown, was not new. She told us little that we did not know before. But it is one thing to read that story as one reads a novel, sitting at one's ease, with the ocean rolling between us and Haworth, and quite another to hear it from the lips of a humble, faithful friend in the very room where the sisters had so often sat.

"Oh, that you were a stenographer!" I

whispered to Saint Katharine. As the talk went on, conventionalities dropped away, the "Miss" seemed a waste of time and breath, and Mrs. Brown spoke of plain Charlotte and Emily and Anne.

"They do say now," she continued, "that literary folk, such as write books themselves, think that Emily wor as much as Charlotte, an' maybe more. But you see we did not know it. Nobody thought it then. Emily had a very mannish mind, more mannish than the others. She kept herself to herself, close and quiet; but, when you could once get at her, she wor *sfree* [as free?] and frank as anybody. She wor shut up, you might say, and silent. She could not talk like other folk. A great worker she wor; and, when sore trouble came, the worse she felt, the harder she worked. You know about Branwell? That wor a great grief; but the day he wor buried she just came home and took off her black bonnet and went to the kitchen to help old Tabby with the dinner, just as if nothing had happened. Yet it wor killing her, and in two months she died herself. She would not have a doctor, though a blind man could see how it wor going; and she would get up and have her clothes on, and do her work till the last morning. It wor dreadful to see her, yet none could say a word. At the very last she whispered to Miss Charlotte that she might send for the doctor. But it wor too late. She went out like a candle. Very soon Anne followed her, and there wor but one where there had been three. Yes, my husband buried them all, every one of them. He wor sexton forty year. He and Branwell were great cronies. That's his portrait." And she pointed proudly to a crude oil painting that hung behind her, stiff and woodeny enough, yet with a certain air of individuality about it that made one sure it was a good likeness. "Branwell painted it."

Judicious questioning led her in due time to Miss Brontë's betrothal and marriage.

"Mr. Brontë would not hear to it at first. He wor dead against it. But she brought him round after a while. It wor kept very still, and it wor a quiet wedding. Mr. Nichols and a friend o' his just slipped across the fields to the church, when no one noticed; and Miss Charlotte she put on her white gown and bonnet and met them there, just as if it were nothing at all."

"She did not go through that little gate and down the path through the graveyard, I hope," I said.

"Oh, no! That little gate wor not used except for the burials. They wor all *carried* through that gate. She went down the outside path by the wall. Miss Wooler wor with her, and her friend Miss Ellen. At the last minute, if you can believe it, Mr. Brontë would not go, and Miss Wooler had to give her away. Hardly a one knew what had happened till they came out. Then she had a-hold of Mr. Nichols' arm. They walked that way up to the parsonage; and Miss Charlotte she wor smiling and wor quite chatty, they said."

Then came details, too personal and too sacred to be recorded here, of the short, blissful wedded life, the swift approach of motherhood, the months of anguish, the untimely death.

"When her father saw her lying dead," she went on, "he said: 'I want you all to know that this was why I opposed the marriage. She was like her mother. I knew she was not strong enough to bear the ills of matrimony.'" (The chances are that he used the word "maternity" rather than "matrimony." But I choose to quote literally.) "Mr. Brontë wor a good one," she added thoughtfully.

"How about the pistol?" I asked.

"It wor not true," she answered very decidedly. "Many a thing wor said that never happened about the pistol (though he may well have fired one, now and again, like any other man) and the cutting up of the wife's silk dress and the spoiling of the children's gay shoes. But these things wor not told till the children were all dead and buried."

A glance at the clock showed that time was flying. We bade Charlotte Brontë Brown and her mother good-by, and made our way to the church. Either there is exceptional narrowness on the part of the Haworth people, or there has been great want of tact and good management on the part of the powers that be. Every stone in the old church seems to have been sacred in the eyes of those who were born, as were their ancestors for many a generation, within its shadow. To them the new church is not the loyal and natural successor of the old, but its uprooter and supplanter. The king is dead, and they cannot yet cry, "Long live the king!" This feeling has been intensified by the removal, which was doubtless necessary, of the bodies of Charlotte and her kin from the spot where they were first interred.

"There are folk who would be glad to sweep every vestige of the Brontés off the face of earth," said an old man, with concentrated bitterness of expression. "They have scattered their very bones."

On the wall of the new church there is a small tablet, with names and dates; and there is a memorial window, the gift of an American, we were told, "to the glory of God, and in pleasant memory of Charlotte Bronté."

We went into the churchyard again, to look at the little private gate through which the dead of the Bronté family had been borne to their graves. We cast another glance at the parsonage windows, but we did not venture to knock at the closed door. After being told a dozen times, by as many different persons, that ungracious repulse was certain, we were not brave enough to take the risk. And we have been sorry for our cowardice ever since!

When, at the close of our visit to Haworth, we reached the station, we found we had still half an hour to spare. A fine-looking, elderly man, a good specimen of a Yorkshire yeoman, was sitting on a bench outside, waiting like ourselves for the train. We asked a question or two about new Haworth, and he one or two about America, and we were friends at once.

"Yes," he said, "I wor born about here. I knew the Brontés well. I saw Miss Charlotte very often, almost every day. She wor nothing to look at. She wor a little thing, little and shy. She did not lift up her eyes. She wor quiet and kept out o' the way. They wor all great," — which seems to be the Haworth word for "gifted," — "all great, every one of them. But, yo' see, we did not know it till they wor dead. That wor it." And then he repeated, with a slow shake of the head, "That wor it; we did not know it till they wor dead." Alas! how often a wider world than that of this Yorkshire town has been compelled to make the same sad confession! It took but a word now and then to draw him out. "Yes, we read the books, here in Yorkshire; and we liked them. Good they wor. But we had no idea who wrote them. Bless yo', nobody ever thought *she* wor Currer Bell!— she that wor so little and shy! There wor one John Greenwood. He kep' a little shop where they used to get their paper to write on. He wor too poor to keep a stock on hand; and many's the time, when they wanted it and he wor out, he would walk to Keithley for it, and be back afore night. Alway and always he wor wondering what the young leddies at the parsonage did wi' so much paper. But, bless my soul! John Greenwood never thought no more'n the rest of us that they were writing *books!* Yo' see, we did not know. That wor it."

VII.

FROM THE BORDER TO INVERNESS.

IT is the little things, the trifles light as air, of which guide-books make no note, the unexpected recognitions, the quaint surprises, that give its greatest charm to travel. We were bending our way northward, and had taken the train, as we supposed, for Melrose, when to our chagrin we found we could go no farther that night than Kelso. The town was quite unknown to us. Neither of our three guide-books so much as mentioned it. We searched the maps, and found a tiny circlet, about half-way between Berwick-on-Tweed and the place of our destination. What manner of place was it? No one seemed able to enlighten our ignorance.

"Primitive enough, no doubt," said one

of us, as she looked out of the car window with a disconsolate air. "But I suppose we can find beds, and perhaps bannocks. Bannocks are the proper thing in Scotland, are they not?"

The truth was, we had set our hearts on spending our first night "Over the Border" at Melrose; and the change of plan was not quite satisfactory.

But there was little time for doubt or questioning. As we sped towards the border, all the hills and streams found voices, and every crag had some tale of the past to tell. The very names were suggestive. Flying along in the gloaming, we stopped for an instant at — was it "Norham," the name that caught my eye as we swept past the station? — And why should a swift vision out of the old romances — a vision of mail-clad knights and haughty barons — rise before me at that word?

It all came to me presently. "Why, this is Norham!" I cried excitedly. "Don't you remember? Norham, where Edward I. met the Lords of Scotland when they made him arbitrator between Robert the Bruce and false John Baliol."

Just at that moment, the guard, running along on the platform outside, spoke through the open window. "Ladies," he said, touching his cap, "this place was celebrated in the border wars. We shall pass the ruins of Norham Castle presently."

Soon we saw it to the right of us, looming up in its hoary grandeur like a ghost in the dim twilight.

We rolled into Kelso, at last. Even our friendly guard was as ignorant as other folk — as ignorant as railroad officials and hotel clerks sometimes are, on the other side of the water. He "had never stopped at Kelso." He "did n't know the place." Was there a good hotel there? Indeed, he could n't say, but it seemed to him he had "heard mention of an inn called The Crossed Keys."

"That sounds rather mediæval and romantic," whispered Saint Katharine. "Do you suppose there is a dungeon under the coffee-room?" Gathering up our belongings, we looked about in quest of adventures and a porter.

Alas! a most commonplace omnibus awaited us. It had not even the musty odour of antiquity to redeem it, but quite dazzled our eyes with its unaccustomed cleanliness and brilliancy, being by all odds the finest carryall we had seen since we left London.

It takes but little to amuse light-hearted travellers, and we laughed heartily at our own three selves (for there were three of us this time) as we presently emerged into a large, well-paved, and well-lighted market-place, on one side of which stood The Crossed Keys, bearing on its heavy door the iron symbols of guardianship. Well might we laugh at the erroneous impression we had formed of the beautiful town of Kelso, which boasts an ancient abbey of its own; Kelso, with its fine roads, its graceful bridges, its museum and library, and its background of wooded hills with the three Eildon peaks in the distance.

As for The Crossed Keys, however, it was primitive enough to be interesting; even though our party of three voted that the breakfast served us the next morning in our pleasant parlour, by a blue-eyed young Scotchman, was the best we had tasted on British soil.

There was a strange exhilaration in the atmosphere that August morning. Or was it from within? — a spiritual essence stronger than wine. Did not the very air we breathed with such delight stir the ivies of Melrose, and Abbotsford, and Dryburgh?

It was but a dozen miles or so to St. Boswell's, whither we went by rail; and there took a carriage for the short two-mile drive to Dryburgh. Alighting on the banks of the Tweed, we crossed the river on a very long, narrow, swaying foot-bridge, under whose piers two young men in tourist costumes were gravely fishing. It was quite safe, with iron railings, and to fall would have been impossible. But the wind blew strongly, and the procedure was a good deal like walking the deck in a gale. Once over, however, we went on, through green and winding ways, to the first lodge, where we stopped to pay toll — "tuppence" — for crossing the bridge, and to receive directions for finding the abbey.

One of us was slightly indisposed that morning, in spite of the delicious air; and crossing that swaying bridge had not helped the matter. She looked ready to commit the crime of fainting. What was to be done? For we had already left the lodge well behind us.

Fortunately a little, low cottage sprang

up out of the shadows by the wayside, and we concluded to make an informal morning call. It was whitewashed on the outside, with scarlet geraniums blooming in the small windows, but inside it was brown and Rembrandtish in tone.

"Isn't it just like a picture?" whispered one of us, as we took a quiet survey before entering.

A wood fire burned in the blackened fireplace, the sticks resting on large iron firedogs. On one side were the small-paned windows, with deep window-sills; on the other, bunks were built into the wall, one above another, sleeping accommodations for the family.

As we appeared in the narrow doorway, a tall, angular woman, with a complexion like leather, and a wide-bordered cap surmounting the black coil of her hair, came forward to receive us. Taking in the situation at a glance, she cried hospitably, while drawing forth a rocking chair, "Oh, coom in, coom in ! Let the leddy coom right in ! There's nane but the bairns in here the morn."

One of the " bairns," a little, red-cheeked, dark-eyed boy about five years old, was curled up in a great arm-chair, on a many-coloured patchwork cushion, intently watching the boiling of a pot over the fire. He looked at us curiously, but not shyly, lifted his hand, smiled, and said something in an unknown tongue — courteous words of greeting, no doubt. Children soon catch the spirit of their elders; and this little fellow's mother could not have been more gracious, or more self-respecting, if she had been Duchess of Buccleugh.

Our invalid was soon conducted upstairs into a low, wide room, with brown rafters, filled with all sorts of household belongings — the odds and ends of many generations. There she was left to herself for half an hour, while the rest of us made friends with the mother and her bairns. The experience taught us one fact not mentioned in the guide-books; viz., that a Scotch peasant-woman may have a guest-chamber in her small cottage, and may gently decline payment from a stranger for the use thereof.

In due time we passed the second lodge, entered our names in the visitors' book, paid our sixpences, and made our way down the narrow, ivy-hedged lane that leads to the abbey, now so picturesque in ruinous solitude. The ruin is indeed almost complete. We did not try to trace out nave, or choir, or transept, but sat there in the sweet morning stillness, hearing the birds sing and communing with tree and flower till we were fully rested.

Then we sought St. Mary's aisle in what was once the north transept of a stately pile, but which the world hardly knows of now save as the burial-place of Walter Scott. There he sleeps, with his wife and son by his side, and Lockhart at his feet.

An iron railing prevents intrusion upon the sacred spot; but seeing some pebbles lying on the pavement within, I put my hand reverently through the grating and gathered them up for friends across the sea who would, I well knew, prize them above rubies.

The works of men's hands, "yea, all of them shall wax old like a garment." Yet near the entrance to the abbey stands a yew-tree, still hale and green in its serene old age; a yew-tree that is older than the abbey itself. What stories could it not tell if it had but a tongue to speak!

Abbotsford is too well known to warrant description here. Suffice it to say that we were permitted to wander at will through the fair chambers that are still haunted by the master's presence, and through the grounds and gardens that he planted. We paused for a moment at the monument erected to the memory of the "twa dogs," Maida and Lufa; and by the half-finished statue of Maurice, the exciseman in "Rob Roy." In the armoury, we lingered long over the curious relics so associated with the works of their former owner, and so indicative of his tastes and character — among them Rob Roy's gun, pouch, and cap; the keys of the Heart of Midlothian, and some strands of golden hair cut from the head of Bonnie Prince Charlie. In a little octagon recess was the death mask.

Perhaps what will be remembered longest is the frieze in the hall entrance, formed wholly of the shields and armorial bearings of the Scottish clans, with this inscription running underneath : —

"These be the Coat Armouries of ye Clannis and men of name quha keepit ye Scottish Marches in ye days of auld. They were worthie in their tyme, and in their defens, God thaim defended."

The drive to Melrose in the sunny afternoon was enchanting as we followed the winding Tweed round the base of the Eildon Hills, three rounded cones, brown and purple with heather. We looked at them curiously, remembering how Michael, the Wizard, had by his dark magic "cleft Eildon Hill in three." It was a fair picture that stamped itself upon our memories that day, — the clear blue sky, the bright sunshine, the sparkling river, the picturesque hills, and at their feet, half buried in foliage, the country-seat of the Duke of Buccleugh — his "hunting-box," so called, — the box being large enough to accommodate a hundred guests.

The Abbey Inn is at the very gate of the abbey; not a stone's throw off. Indeed, one can hardly help believing that it encroaches upon the site of the ancient nave. It is a pity that Melrose does not stand like Fountains Abbey, isolated in lonely grandeur. But as imagination takes hold of and reclothes and repeoples the majestic ruin, one has no room for regrets of any kind. The historic and poetic associations are so rich that they become overpowering. To stand where the heart of the Bruce lies buried, on the very spot where the high altar once lifted its imposing splendour, all bathed in the glorious, many-coloured light that streamed in through the 'flamboyant traceries of that marvellously beautiful eastern window, and then to lift one's eyes and see, not six feet off, the tomb of the Douglases, where lies *the* Douglas whom Harry Hotspur slew at Otterburn, is surely enough to make the most sluggish heart beat faster than its wont. Here, as everywhere in the old world, it is less the thing seen than the thing suggested that stirs one.

Melrose is beyond description. Surely its arches were bent, and its mighty columns — bundles of lances bound together by garlands — were reared in days when time was naught and human endeavour was of small moment. What manner of men were they — these builders in what we are pleased to call the "dark ages"? Dark perhaps, because the morning of our boasted civilization had not yet dawned. The delicacy and grace of the carvings, whether in the frieze of the cloisters, or in the capitals of the pillars, the corbels, and the keystones of the roof, are incomparable. Rose and lily, thistle, thorn, and fern, kale and oak leaves, with countless other forms of unapproachable loveliness, are reproduced in the solid stone with a fidelity to nature that takes one's breath away. Just above the foliated capital of the centre pillar in the north transept, is carved a hand holding in its slender fingers a few flowers. Of this hand Lockhart says that " were it cut off and placed with the Elgin marbles, it would be kissed by the cognoscenti as one of the finest of them all."

Passing out by the grand south entrance, we found ourselves in the graveyard, from the southeast corner of which the best view of the building as a whole is to be obtained.

At this point the eye takes in at once the singular beauty of the flying buttresses, the glorious arches, the grand east window, and the central tower.

Midway across this field of the dead we found a sunken grave, marked by a little red stone which bore this singular inscription : —

> "The Earth goeth on the Earth
> Glistering like gold;
> The Earth goeth to the Earth
> Sooner than it wold;
> The Earth builds on the Earth
> Castles and towers;
> The Earth says to the Earth
> All shall be ours."

The stone is very old. On the other side was the name of the silent sleeper, "Jane Ramsey," and the remains of a date that time had blotted out. I fancied her a young girl; for did not the stone tell us dust had returned to dust "sooner than it wold"? Unfortunately for this theory, however, the old seem, as a rule, quite as anxious to live as are their grandchildren.

Not far from "Jane" lies Thomas Purdie, "Wood Forester at Abbotsford"; and the stone is erected in "grateful remembrance" of an old servant, "by Sir Walter Scott, Bart."

We lingered long in the dim twilight, feeling rather than seeing the witchery of the place, the magic, the beauty of it all. Then we went to bed, but not to sleep. For who could sleep beneath the towers of Melrose, when he knew the moon would rise about midnight?

My room overlooked the abbey — was almost in it, in fact. My bed was in front of the window, and I had only to lift the curtain to behold the glorious pageant as th full moon slowly rose, flooding choir and chancel, nave and cloister, with a clear white light that was almost like day.

"The broken arches were black in night,
And each shafted oriel glimmered white,

Where the cold light's uncertain shower
Streamed on the ruined central tower."

As I gazed, shadowy figures seemed to glide from column to column, from arch to arch. Cowled monks stole down the old staircase; they emerged from the "steel-clenched postern door," they knelt before the high altar. Is that Father Eustacious, the last abbot of St. Mary's? Is the place alive again with warmth and colour, the breath of incense, the stately splendour of solemn ceremonials?

Hark! a tolling bell strikes the hours,— a weird, unearthly sound that sends a shiver through the soul. It is the very bell that called to prayer four centuries ago.

Many good things have come into my life, but I count among the best of them those midnight, moonlit hours at Melrose.

Then followed rare, enchanted weeks in Edinboro' the Proud, Edinboro' the Beautiful. The tourist, and there is more than one, who says she should not be proud and is not beautiful, has been most unfortunate. Either he was soul-sick, or body-sick, or he had atrocious weather, or he did not stay long enough for the fair city to reveal her charms to him.

"Shall I tell you how your countrymen and countrywomen, for the most part, *do* Edinboro'?" asked a stately Scotch matron with laughter in her eye and voice. "Very well! They alight at the station. They get into cabs — one cab, two cabs, fifty cabs, according to the size of the party. They drive through a few streets; they go up to the castle, and in the twinkling of an eye are whisked from dungeon to tower. Into the cabs again, and down High Street and the Canongate to Holyrood. They glance at St. Giles, and the Tolbooth. They look up at Arthur's Seat, and down from Calton Hill to the Forth. They stop a minute at the Scott monument. They run into a shop and buy a pebble, or a cairngorm. Then to the station again, and off they whirl. They have seen Edinboro'. Did I tell you about the young man who went to Rosslyn? No? Very well, then. He drove out with a party of friends, and when they got to the chapel actually refused to leave the carriage. 'Why should he alight?' he asked. 'He didn't come all the way to Europe to see a parcel of old ruins,'—not having studied his little red book enough to show that Rosslyn was *not* a ruin. Much good travel does such folk," she added impatiently. "Why doesn't Fate give their chance to the other sort?"

And remembering sundry appreciative souls who would give more than the half of their respective kingdoms for the "chance" this callow youth was wasting, my heart echoed the question.

But the charmed days could not last. We had done all the orthodox things and many that were not orthodox. We had not only seen that grand old pile of embodied history yclept the Castle, but we had dreamed of it, sleeping in its hoary shadow, as it were, night after night. We had trodden the storied ways of beautiful Holyrood. We had stood in the window from which John Knox thundered his anathemas. We had climbed Salisbury Craig, and, sighing because Arthur's Seat — its crest, that is — was too high for us and we could not attain unto it, we had looked down on the towered and turreted city sleeping at our feet, and afar off beyond Leith to the blue waters of the Forth. Did we not become familiar with "the hills beyond Pentland"? Did we not see the fishwives of Newhaven? And on one never-to-be-forgotten day, we followed the serpentine windings of the Firth of Forth, past fishing villages and hamlets sleeping in the sun; past crag and cairn, crumbling tower, ivied ruin, and lofty monument; past quiet homes, half hidden under sheltering trees; past stately castles and historic piles; past church and abbey, school and hospital, until at length, as we neared Stirling, so swiftly did the steamer wheel and veer in its tortuous channel that the castle on one storied height and the Wallace monument on another seemed playing hide-and-seek with us, and we were fain to believe there were two castles and two monuments.

But why go on with the inventory? Wherever we went, whatever we saw or did, one figure walked beside us by night and by day. Walter Scott is the soul of Edinboro'. His presence pervades the streets and the very air. It is fitting that, as the years go by, he should sit upon his marble throne, under that canopy of carven stone, with the creations of his genius above and around him as a holy guard, in the very heart of the city of his love. You see his face everywhere. Indeed the face of the queen is not more familiar to the people of London than is that of Walter Scott to the people of Edinboro'.

On that last morning we went again up Castle Street to Number Thirty-nine, — the home of the magician for twenty-six years; the home of his prime, where in one single year he wrote " Peveril of the Peak," " Quentin Durward," and " St. Ronan's Well." Number One, North Charlotte Street, was not far off, the occasional home of " Pet Marjorie," from whence she came to the Twelfth Night supper at Castle Street, brought in the sedan chair by Duncan Roy and Tougald. It was easy to see it all — the little seven-year-old darling, "all in white, and her eyes gleaming, and Scott bending over her in ecstasy." It required no great stretch of fancy to see the opening of the " big ha' door," and to hear a gay voice cry, " I can make nothing of ' Waverley ' to-day. I'll awa' to Marjorie. Come wi' me, Maida, you thief," as the tall figure strode down the street with a shepherd's plaid over its shoulder.

It was in the garden back of the Castle

Street house that poor faithful Camp was buried, the turf above him smoothed by his master's own hand.

It is the fashion in some quarters to say that the world has outgrown the author of "Waverley," that "nobody reads him." Perhaps so, — though the statistics of public libraries do not attest this. But he lives and breathes in Scotland. You can scarcely say of him that "being dead he yet speaketh"; for it is impossible to think of him as dead, even though he has every mountain for a monument.

Saint Katharine and I resolved ourselves into a committee of two. Should we go up to Inverness "first class," or "second"? The committee referred the question to the stately matron and her fair daughters. "You would better go first class." was the decision. "It is a long, hard journey up to Inverness, very tiresome if taken in one day."

The British idea of distance is very amusing to an American. A trip of six or eight hours is a "long, hard journey," to be attempted only under protest, and with more impedimenta in the shape of wraps, rugs, and air cushions, than would suffice for an outing across the continent from New York to San Francisco. But we were so far influenced as to bestow ourselves and our portmanteaux in a first-class compartment, thereby paying exactly double for the privilege of sitting on plush instead of rep, and having an extra arm to lean against. That was about all the difference we were able to discover, speaking generally, between first and second class cars, though we made many trials of both.

Stirling was an old story. So was Dumblane, where we looked, as we had looked before, for "Fair Jessie," but failed to find her — though it is quite possible we saw her great-granddaughter in a straw hat and scarlet jacket; said jacket being in close proximity to another jaunty bit of scarlet that was gay with gold lace and bright buttons.

After leaving Dumblane we were on new ground. Are there ghostly houses, I wonder? Not houses that are haunted by ghosts, but houses that are ghosts themselves? Not a stone is left of the old monastery of the Black Friars at Perth. But surely its shadowy phantom rose before us, and within its unsubstantial chambers we saw James the First, wise king, soldier-poet, loyal gentleman, in his very "habit as he lived." Brave Catharine Douglas, too, was there, barring the door against his pursuers with her frail right arm; and pale Joanna, stilling her trembling maids.

Below us on either side as we crossed the Tay stretched the fair "Inches of Perth," smiling in the level sunshine. Apparently they have quite forgotten how once on their broad meadows thirty men of Clan Chattan fought thirty of Clan Kay, until the river ran with blood, and but twelve men, and they sorely wounded, were left out of the whole sixty.

Then up we climbed through the heart of the Highlands, mountain towering above mountain, and the scenery growing more and more vividly picturesque, till we reached the wild pass of Killiecrankie, just beyond which a rude stone marks the spot where Claverhouse fell. How or why he ever allowed General MacKay to loiter through the easily defended pass, where the very spirits of the woods and the mountains waited to join forces with the "Bonnets of Bonnie Dundee," must ever be a mystery. The battle was fought in the open valley beyond.

It was nearing sunset when we passed Blair-Athole, that loveliest of Highland hamlets, with the many-turreted castle of the earls of Athole rising out of the trees on the hillside, and the old church of Blair, the burial-place of Dundee, just beyond it. The scene may not always be so fair as it was that August afternoon, when the purple of the heather, blending with the soft olives and browns of ferns and mosses, clothed every mountain from base to summit, and all were enwrapped in the golden haze that was the forerunner of the sunset. But as we saw it, it was beautiful beyond description. The shadows grew deeper as we lost sight of Ben Vrackie. Look, Saint Katharine! Is that the shade of Macbeth stalking along in the gloaming? Surely here "foul whisperings are abroad," for lo! proud Dunsinane towers on one side, and on the other Burnam Hill, robed to its crown in stately evergreens.

A tall gray monument rose to the right, crowning a slight elevation. "To the honour of the 'Wolf of Badenock,' ladies," explained a courtly Highland gentleman who shared our compartment. "You are now in the very heart of the old clans. There are the MacIntoshes, over there the MacDonalds, and farther on the Camerons, the Gordons, the Frasers, and many another name doubtless as familiar to you as to me." As he got off at Kencraig, and was met by friends, as well as by retainers to whose care he consigned a hamper that had been stowed away under the seat, we had strong suspicions that our courteous *camarade du voyage* was himself "one of the MacIntoshes."

At the next station two bright-faced laddies in Highland caps and shooting jackets, laden with rods and creels and all manner of fishing toggery, swept in upon us like a pair of young whirlwinds. Very well-mannered whirlwinds they were, however, not forgetting to make graceful salutation as they established themselves in comfortable quarters. Their baskets were suspiciously empty, and it was doubtless the anticipation of joys to come that made their young faces so radiant, and kept them in a subdued gale till they left us a few stations farther on.

Night fell all too soon. Yet we had passed the best of the Highlands before it came; and what with the glory of the heather, the glory of the mountains, the glory of cloud and sky, we were tired out, and were willing at last to shut our eyes, while our souls chanted the Te Deum, — "All the earth doth worship thee, the Father everlasting."

At ten o'clock we reached Inverness.

VIII.
TO CAWDOR CASTLE AND CULLODEN MOOR.

FOR four weeks Scotland had given us of her best. We had had the glory of the heather, the glory of the lakes, the glory of mountain and cloud and sky, to say nothing of that other glory of storied castles, ruins magnificent in their decay, and palaces whose every stone could speak. And we had not seen so much as a hint of a Scotch mist, or a drop of rain!

But on the 22d of August we found the skies overcast and a storm impending. We compared notes, and consulted the most genial and painstaking host in the United Kingdom. Certainly we had not come up there to be daunted by a little rain; and most certainly, too, if we were to see Cawdor Castle and Culloden Moor at all, we must see them that day. It was not one of the coach days, either. The porter came to the fore to give his advice. The leddies could perhaps get a machine, and go by themselves. "A machine?" We opened wide eyes, and then and there added something to our store of knowledge; namely, the fact that in Highland dialect a "machine" is any sort of a "trap" in which human beings can ride. Would we have a machine for the round trip, twenty-eight miles? Indeed we would.

The machine, in this instance, proved to be a light open wagonette for one horse; the driver in front, and seats for two, facing each other, behind. Unrolling our mackintoshes for the first time since we landed at Liverpool, in June, we took our umbrellas, and climbed into the small vehicle. Our host put in wraps and rugs enough for the supply of a regiment, and off we started just as the rain began to fall, declaring to each other that it was great fun, — as it was, if fun is ever synonymous with pure, unadulterated enjoyment.

For anything more delightful can hardly be conceived than that drive in the soft, warm rain, that was in itself a luxury after the long drought, — along the curving shores of the Moray Firth, through lovely wooded recesses where the dripping branches met above our heads, between hedge-rows where all sweet wild things were growing together in riotous confusion, holly, and wild rose, and ivy, and bramble, twining their arms about each other and dancing as if for very joy, and beside banks all matted with heather, so deliciously pink when seen near at hand, so royally purple when it stretches afar over moorland and mountain. All along the way bluebells swaying in the wind and rain swung their perfect chalices, and tiny pink and yellow flowers, unknown to us, poised like butterflies on slender stalks to keep them company. Here and there stately rowan-trees flamed beside the road, their great trusses of scarlet berries burning like torches in the dark emerald of their leaves.

The roads were perfect, as level as a floor; not a rut, nor a stone, nor a hillock big enough to make a "cradle-hole," and no mud even in the rain. Well, Great Britain has been building her roads for eighteen hundred years, and she had the Romans to teach her how and set her a good example. Perhaps ours will be as fine when we have worked at them as long.

We drove up at length, after much circumambulation and many devious windings, before Ye Cawdor Arms, a little quaint old inn at the junction of the highway with the lane that leads to the castle. It was a most primitive establishment in which to look for entertainment for man and beast. The low stone walls had lost, if they had ever possessed, the garniture of ivy that so often makes the hovel more picturesque than the palace, and stood forth in all their unveiled nakedness. A few scarlet runners on poles made a bit of intense brightness in one corner. On the opposite corner of the house, just under the low eaves, a weather-beaten sign displayed the latest attempt at emblazoning the arms of the House of Cawdor. Apparently it had been painted over and over again by a hundred successive generations. The inn itself looked old enough to have given food and shelter to King Duncan's retainers, when he made his unfortunate visit to the Thane of Cawdor.

It had stopped raining by this time, and, leaving our waterproofs and dripping umbrellas at the inn, we walked down the lane to the ivy-covered arch of the gateway leading to the castle. Near it was a small cottage, too unpretentious to be called a lodge, in the door of which stood an old woman, curtsying. Did we wish to call on the leddies o' the family? No, we were strangers. We only wished permission to see the castle, we answered. "But ye maun ha' tickets for *that*," she said. Here was a dilemma. But it proved a very simple matter. They could be had at the post-office for a "saxpenny" each; and our driver, who, having looked after the wellbeing of his horse, now stood at a little distance, peering over the lichen-covered stone wall into the dark flowing rivulet beyond it, could readily obtain them. The "saxpennies" were for the poor. Meanwhile, what wonder that we were seized with a sudden conviction that our feet were cold?

"May we come in and warm our feet by your fire?" I asked.

"Ay, ay, coom in, coom in, and sit ye doon," she said heartily, as she ushered us in, and wiped two spotlessly clean chairs before offering them to us. Such a queer little place as it was! The outside door was of some rich, dark, polished wood, studded with brass knobs, but in it lay all the splendour of the establishment. The walls were so low I could have touched the ceiling with my hand. The stone floor, the table, and the two or three chairs, one of which was adorned with a cushion covered with worsted patchwork, had been scoured till they were white. In one corner stood a narrow bed, entirely covered by a pointed canopy of some faded pink stuff. Over the blackened, smoke-stained fireplace were a couple of shelves, not for bric-à-brac, but filled with dishes and household utensils. A kettle hummed over the fire, which was certainly built on an economical scale, considering the dampness of the day. On the one broad window-seat lay a book, brown leather and well-thumbed, which was evidently a Bible. In the chimney-corner, a cat purred softly. It was like a chapter out of some story of humble, pious poverty, — little fire, little cat, well-worn Bible, and all.

The old woman was interested in her

visitors. We had come a long ways, — from Lunnon, or from furren parts, mebbe, to see the old castle?

Yes; we had come from over the sea, all the way from America.

As usual, we had found the "open sesame." Everywhere, in England and Scotland alike, America had been the magic key that unlocked all doors.

"Ye can't get in till three o'clock," she said, excitedly. "But if ye only tell the housekeeper *that*, she'll let ye in noo!"

We preferred, however, notwithstanding this encouragement, to wait till the regular hour of admittance. As we started to go back to the inn for our luncheon, I slipped a bit of silver into the old woman's wrinkled hand. She would have refused it, had I not insisted, crying, "Ye needn't to do it; ye needn't to do it! But God bless ye, and mak' ye rich, and bring ye safe hame to yer ain people."

This was so remarkable that I at once

"made a note on't." And I wish here to solemnly record the fact that there were two persons in the United Kingdom who actually objected to receiving a proffered shilling. In both cases they were not ablebodied men, but poor, lonely old women.

Ye Cawdor Arms does not provide very luxuriously for its guests. But we had our luncheon, such as it was, at the same table with a young man who looked like a student on his vacation tramp. As he slowly ate his cold meat and bread and cheese, and sipped his single glass of wine, he read from a book lying open beside his plate, with one hand resting half the time on the head of a beautiful Scotch collie. The master kept his distance; but the dog, after making a deliberate survey, drew nearer and nearer, and finally laid his great head on my knee, while his eloquent brown eyes begged for a share of our portion of the feast. He got it.

We started for the castle at last, entering

in under the ivied archway, and going up the broad gravelled road, with smooth green lawns, dotted with stately forest trees, stretching far to the left.

"'This castle hath a pleasant seat; the air nimbly and sweetly recommends itself unto our gentle senses,'" quoted Saint Katharine, as we crossed the rusty drawbridge over the moat, and entered through what had once been a portcullis into a small, square court, from which steps descended on either side unto other courts. Right in front of us, facing the drawbridge, was a mounted cannon, with the conical heap of balls beside it. We knew that in spite of all these warlike preparations there must be a hospitable bell somewhere; and failing to discover it above, we went down into the lower right-hand court, where we found it, and the door of entrance.

An exquisite young Adonis in livery appeared, — Jeemes being generally a more elegant man than his master. Certainly we could see the castle, from three to five. But — looking at his watch — it still wanted five minutes to three.

We begged pardon. Our watches must be at fault. But, meanwhile, might we be permitted to walk in the grounds?

We might; and he would himself notify the housekeeper of our desires.

We crossed the drawbridge again, nothing loath to wander about the place, so still and peaceful now, and to look down the long vistas leading into the adjoining forest. Presently a schoolboy, with slate and books, came out of the castle, and hurried down a shaded lane to a building near by. Soon two young women in walking costume, with tartans picturesquely draped over their shoulders, and carrying small baskets, passed by us, on the traditional errand of mercy, no doubt.

"Port wine and beef-tea in one basket, no doubt," said I, "and a flannel petticoat in the other."

Then, as we turned towards the house again, we met two gentlemen, one of whom, it was evident, from his air of proprietorship and at-homeness, was Lord Campbell.

"'The Thane of Cawdor lives, a prosperous gentleman' still, if one may judge from appearances," I remarked to Saint Katharine, as he lifted his cap, and we went our separate ways.

The housekeeper, a handsome, middle-aged woman, in cashmere gown and pretty cap, received us at the door with such an air of smiling hospitality that we felt at home at once. Cawdor Castle is almost the only one of the really old castles — that is, those that have not been thoroughly made over and modernized — that is still used as a family residence. We were first taken into the dining-room, where the table, not yet fully cleared, showed that luncheon was just over. It was a pleasant, low-ceiled room, completely hung with old needle-work tapestry. The only modern thing in or about it was the carved wooden mantelpiece, which was put in by the present earl, and bears his crest and those of his four sisters, with the date of the room, 1510.

From thence we went to the kitchen, whose walls, many feet thick, had been redolent with the odours of roasting mutton and venison as far back as the fourteenth century. The enormous fireplace that nearly fills one end is unaltered, and before it, or in it, the family cooking is done to this day. For the help of the cook there is some odd machinery, still in good working order and in daily use, though as old as the chimney itself, by which the heat of the fire turns and regulates the spit. The upper end of the great room is hewn out of the solid rock, floor, walls, and ceiling being of the same mass of stone. Long tables extended down the middle throughout the whole length, and half a dozen maids, busy with pans, pots, and scrubbing-brushes, glanced at us curiously as we passed by. Familiarity breeds contempt; and there is small doubt that they marvelled under their caps at the interest, or curiosity, that brought so many questioning eyes into their old kitchen.

A short winding passage and a flight of steps led us to the dungeon. It is not a bad place, as dungeons go, having more light, air, and space than most of them. Still, the sound of the heavy iron door swinging to, with a clang, upon its rusty hinges, must have been anything but agreeable to the poor captives upon whom it has so often closed. It was a hard thing to realize, with that kindly, smiling face beside us, instead of a warder in coat-of-mail. In the middle of the dungeon, like the central column of a chapter-house, rose the trunk of a large hawthorn-tree. "There is a curious story about this old tree, which is older than the castle itself," said the housekeeper, laying her hand upon it. "The founder of the house was looking for a place to build upon, when a saint, or an angel (it doesn't matter which), appeared to him, and told him he must build upon whatever spot an ass laden with gold should stop three times successively. Shortly afterward, an ass weighed down with treasures persisted in stopping three times in the shade of this hawthorn-tree. And so, you see, we have our castle, which was built around it."

To establish at once the principle of believing whatever is told you, wonderfully enhances the interest of travel. We had done this at the very outset of our pilgrimage, and of course believed this bit of mediæval history implicitly. But we may perhaps be forgiven if we venture to wonder whether the ass and his gold belonged to the founder, or to his dearest enemy.

"Now you must see King Duncan's

room," said our pleasant guide, leading the way to the tower stairs. The climbing of steep, narrow, winding ways, worn into such great hollows that one can hardly feel sure of a foothold, is, to put it mildly, not as easy as going up in an elevator. But reflecting it was but once in a lifetime, I plucked up my courage, and gallantly followed in the wake of the small procession. After ascending two or three flights, we entered a large square room, with two windows commanding a wide and pleasant outlook. It was plainly furnished, containing a canopied bed, with chintz drapery drawn up and carefully spread over the pillows, after the inevitable Scotch-English fashion, a table, a chest of drawers, and a few chairs.

"Now tell me truly," said I, — for, sad as it is to say it, there is sometimes a limit to the credulity of the most conscientious traveller, — "*was* King Duncan ever in this room? The castle figures in the play, but was the king murdered here?"

"No," she said, "as you ask me frankly, I must say he was not. This castle is not as old as the date of Macbeth. But Shakespeare chose it as the scene of the murder, and out of deference to that fact the family has always kept up the tradition, and called this the Duncan room."

The decorations of the apartment, if so they could be called, were truly unique. The space above the fireplace, in which was a pair of huge iron fire-dogs, was completely covered by a charcoal sketch done upon the white wall. The three weird sisters were brewing their unholy witch-broth in a great caldron, while the flames struggled with the clouds of smoke, out of which the uncanny faces peered. On one side of the fire, a black cat humped her back, and hissed at a serpent coiled and just ready to dart, on the other side. On the left of the fireplace was a life-sized figure of Macbeth, with hair on end and dagger drawn, staring with horror in his eyes at the real and truly bed, in which Duncan, no doubt, was supposed to be lying. On the wall at the foot of the bed was Lady Macbeth, tragical to the last degree, urging him on to the commission of the bloody deed. Rough as they were, there was spirit in the drawings. Evidently a party of merry young people had amused themselves with this attempt to make the Duncan room truly Shakespearian.

The rest of the party went up several flights farther, while I stayed below with Duncan and the witches. They saw the window from which Simon Fraser, Lord Lovat, was let down in a basket during the Jacobite wars, — escaping then, only to be beheaded afterwards; and the loopholes through which, in the good old times, melted lead was poured like coals of fire upon the heads of besieging foes.

Pleasanter far than this was it to look down from their airy perch into the forest, where they could see the lovely woodland paths stretching on and on. The great estate runs thirty miles in one direction.

We were agreeably surprised by being taken into the family rooms, the private apartments, to say much of which here would be a breach of trust and hospitality. But some jewel-lovers amongst us envied my lord the magnificent gems that sparkled on his dressing-table. One daintily furnished chamber, with the open Prayer-Book on its own small table, the text for the day on the wall, the basket of needlework, the well-worn companionable books lying within convenient reach of the low, deep-cushioned chair that awaited the coming of its mistress in front of the smouldering fire, left on some of our minds a most pleasant impression of gentle, refined, studious, thoughtful girlhood.

The great drawing-room was as homelike a place as one need wish to see, — a long, low-ceiled, tapestry-hung apartment, with the fire of logs on the broad hearth burning low, the sunshine streaming in, and flowers in profusion everywhere; a room for use, not show, for on a little table where some one had been mounting photographs, the sponge, bowl of water, and mucilage bottle were all ready for further operations. From the walls the ancient lords and ladies of Cawdor looked down on the pretty, peaceful scene. I wondered if they did not think they had had a hard time of it themselves, in the far-away centuries full of turmoil and bloodshed.

"Have the lords of Cawdor always been Campbells?" I inquired.

"Oh, no," was the answer. "But long ago the sole heiress of the house of Cawdor married a Campbell, — one of the Argyles, you know," she added confidentially, — "and so the family name was changed."

Soon after this we passed out under the portcullis and over the drawbridge, down the broad, smooth walk, and through the green archway into the country lane again, and our visit to Cawdor Castle was over.

It was not actually raining again, but it was still dark and lowering. The young Highlander who had charge of our "machine" looked dubiously at the clouds, as we resumed our seats. By a short cut across country, we could be home in an hour. If we went round by way of Culloden, we would surely be caught in the rain.

"And there's nothing to see there, anyhow," he said. "Just an empty field."

But the nothingness of Culloden Moor was exactly what we wanted to see, and we went on.

Nature had harmonized charmingly with all our doings through the whole summer. Sunshine would have been out of place that afternoon. As we approached Culloden, the clouds grew darker and deeper. The dull gray mists lay damp and heavy on the barren moor. The silent hills were blotted out. The sky hung so low it seemed as if we could touch it; and it and the mists shut us in. There was nothing left of the whole wide world but the moor of Culloden, and we were the only living creatures in it. Not a bird sang; not a grouse, nor a rabbit, resented our intrusion upon its solitudes.

First we passed, lying in a field to our left, but very near the road, an immense gray bowlder, lettered "Cumberland, 1746." From this stone the "Butcher Duke" commanded the field, on that April day when the last hope of the Stuarts was crushed. An eighth of a mile farther on, the horse stopped.

"This is the 'Field of the Dead,'" said our young cavalier, half under his breath. He had not wanted to come, but now that he was here the scene and the hour took hold upon him as upon us. The poet has set his sign manual upon all things here in this Old World. It is quite probable that this young fellow did not know he was quoting; but half the schoolboys in America have "spoken" —

"Lochiel, Lochiel, beware of the day
  When the Lowlands shall meet thee in battle array,
  For the *Field of the Dead* rushes red on my sight,
  And the clans of Culloden are scattered in flight."

We got out of the wagonette silently, and walked reverently across the field, still sown with ridges, perceptibly greener than the rest, where the dead were buried in trenches, to a rough gray stone near the outer wall on the left. It was on the very outskirts of the field, and on the other side of the crumbling, moss-grown barricade a few stunted trees and shrubs kept watch and guard.

The stone bore this inscription, rudely cut: —

WELL
OF THE DEAD. HERE THE CHIEF
OF THE CLAN MACGILLIVRAYS
FELL.

Farther down the field was another stone, marked thus: —

CLANS.
MACINTOSH.
MACLEAN.
MACLAUCHLAN.
MACGILLIVRAY.
HIGHLANDERS.

Others, still farther down, were inscribed, severally, "Cameron," "Stewart of Appin," "Fraser."

The stones were all of the roughest description. They looked as if they had been hewn out with the head of a battle-axe, and lettered as rudely. But they were so in keeping with the place, and with the strong, rough natures of the fiercely loyal clansmen who fell at Culloden, that they were more impressive than the most imposing of monuments. On the top of many of the stones kindly hands had laid sprays of their own pink heather. Two only had been overlooked, "Cameron" and "Stewart of Appin." We placed our offering of heather on these also, and then crossed the road to the cairn on the opposite side.

I cannot give the dimensions of this great heap of stones, very slightly conical, if indeed it is conical at all, and flat on top. It is entirely devoid of ornament, this immense sombre cairn, built of the common rounded pebbles lying broadcast on the moor. On one side is an inscription, guarded by an iron grating; for the vandal, like death, has all times and places for his own. It runs thus: —

"Battle of Culloden was fought on this moor 16th April, 1746. The graves of the gallant Highlanders who fought for Scotland and Prince Charlie are marked by the names of their clans."

"By the names of their clans." No separate glory, no distinctive honour, not even a record on a memorial stone, for the warriors who fell at Culloden.

The English are buried near the Cumberland stone. One mile farther on, a slab inscribed "King's Stables" shows where the English army was quartered after the battle.

Right or wrong, good or bad, weak or wicked, by some strong fascination the unfortunate Stuarts hold the hearts of mankind. Bonnie, sunny-haired Prince Charlie is too picturesque a figure to be speedily blotted from the page of history. Peace to his ashes, and long may the purple bells of the heather ring their soft chimes above the dust of his unforgotten braves.

We lingered as long as we dared, and then drove on to Inverness. Just as we entered the town a burst of sunshine greeted us. The beautiful river Ness shone, and danced, and sparkled; rejuvenated birds, thinking spring had come again, poured floods of music from hedge and thicket; and by the time we reached the hotel not a cloud was to be seen.

Smiling, deft-handed Scotch lassies took our wet wraps to the kitchen to be dried. In a trice a fire blazed brightly on our hearth; dinner was served, the dear home letters were brought us, and two happy women settled themselves for an evening of quiet content.

"Saint Katharine," said I, "this has been a day to remember."

IX.
AN ENCHANTED DAY.

"HOT water, mem, and the 'bus leaves at seven," said a soft voice at the door.

"Are you awake, Saint Katharine?" I called. "Do you hear? *Must* we leave Inverness to-day?"

"Yes," she answered, sleepily, to all three questions. "We must. But do you suppose that when we get to heaven we can stay as long as we want to? We have not been to the castle yet."

"Don't bother your blessed head about that," I said consolingly. "The castle is frightfully modern, and it is only a prison, at the best. Nothing is worth looking at over here that is not older than the seventeenth century. Is your portmanteau packed?"

The omnibus was soon announced; but

early as it was, — and seven o'clock is very early in Scotland, — we found our genial host waiting to escort us to the steamer by which we were to go down the Caledonia Canal. Presently we were whirling away through the sunlit, silent streets and over the sparkling river, on our way to the dock of the pretty little Glengarry. As we crossed the bridge, we looked up for the last time, not so much to the castle as to its site on the storied hill. For there Macbeth and his proud queen had dwelt, and there, in some dark chamber of the old eleventh-century castle, that once stood there, there can be little doubt that gentle King Duncan was foully slain. Malcolm Caen-More, he of the " Big Head," razed it to the ground in his filial vengeance, and builded in its stead another and a finer one, where he and fair Margaret Atheling held court for many a day. This, in its turn, was blown up by the troops of Bonnie Prince Charlie in 1746, and number three, the present castle, is a court-house and a jail.

It was a glorious morning, clear and cool, with the bluest of skies, and sunshine that transfigured whatever it touched. There was a merry stir and bustle on board the small craft, but even before we were fairly off order had succeeded chaos, and the passengers, singly, in pairs, or in groups, but all, like John Gilpin, "on pleasure bent," had chosen their seats and established themselves for the day. The comfortable, large-windowed cabins accommodated many; but most of us preferred the upper deck, from which we could watch the long, changeful panorama as it unrolled before us. For the Caledonia Canal, despite its prosaic name, is but a connecting link between a series of surpassingly lovely lochs, running through the Highlands, in almost a direct line, from Inverness to Oban.

For miles after leaving its dock, the little steamer wound its way between green banks, the canal following so closely every bend and curve of the river Ness, which was here scarcely wider than itself, as to seem its veritable shadow or double. The effect was very singular. They were so near each other, and there was so little that was artificial in the appearance of the latter, with its environment of reeds and rushes and the varied outline of its banks, that it was hard to say which was river and which was canal. Just below Inverness we passed the new cemetery, on a hillside sloping to the shore. Trees and flowers, green turf and golden sunshine, made God's-acre beautiful that morning, and we caught glimpses of granite columns and of sculptured marbles. Over one small grave a white-winged angel poised lightly, bearing aloft a flaming torch. The sunlight, streaming down upon it, kindled it as with fire from heaven.

But not for life nor death did our pretty Glengarry pause; and on we swept through little Loch Dockfour into Loch Ness, the longest link in the chain of lakes, and averaging but one mile and a half in breadth. Long and narrow as it is, it has depth enough and to spare, and it never freezes. Little cared the merry passengers whether it did or no, as we stopped for a moment at Urquhart, and saw jutting out into the loch, on a bold peninsula, the ruins of Urquhart Castle. A truncated tower, ivy-mantled to its summit, and with many loop-holes in and out of which the wandering vines creep as they will, and some low crumbling walls, are all that is left of its ancient strength and splendour. A few miles farther down, and we landed at Foyers. There, it was said, omnibuses would be in waiting, to convey such of the passengers as did not care for so long a walk to the falls of Foyers. The boat would wait for us an hour. But the enterprising inhabitants must have made up their minds that the average tourist is a pedestrian.

Just one nondescript vehicle waited at the little pier; and it was filled and whirling away down the road with the first comers long before the rest of us had left the boat. There was a rush for tickets, and then by twos, and threes, and half-dozens, a boatload of people hurried off in the direction of the falls.

"Go on, Saint Katharine," I said, "and see the show if you can. The attempt, even, is beyond my powers."

I followed, very much at my leisure. To see the falls was a matter of small account. But just once in a lifetime to have a few blessed moments all to one's self in those sweet, wild Highland solitudes, — would not that be worth the having? Fate granted me a full half-hour. The crowd passed by me; the footfalls, the gay voices, the peals of laughter, died away. At my left, a narrow path wound up the heights and through the woods to the falls. Before me, the level road stretched on and on.

Sheer cliffs, not bare and desolate, but mantled by all manner of creeping growths, towered on one side. On the other, behind a screen of trees, brightened here and there by the scarlet berries of the rowan, or mountain ash, the beautiful lake shone in the sun.

It was about ten o'clock. The air was fresh, yet warm, and spicy with the breath of the sweet-ferns. At a little distance, a gate in a hedge-row led into a descending lane, fern-bordered and thickly shaded. It was very enticing, and I tried the latch. Alas, it was fastened! There is always a flaming sword before the gate of Paradise — or, if not a sword, its equivalent — to keep us out. Yet why seek for anything better than the best? Paradise was all around me. Now and then a bird, forgetting that springtime and love were over, trilled softly. Butterflies, black and golden, fluttered in the sun, and held special rendezvous wherever the brown earth in the roadway still kept the moisture of the dews. Everything seemed strangely familiar; cranesbill and buttercups bloomed by the wayside, and in the tangled thickets brakes and ferns jostled each other precisely as in rocky Green Mountain pastures. I looked at my watch, and knew that just then the same sun that shone on me in that sweet sylvan solitude was rising over Killington and Pico, three thousand miles away, — kindling the mountaintops with sudden glory, and filling all the fair valleys with radiant light. Nature was chanting the same Te Deum there as here, — "All the earth doth worship thee, the Father everlasting."

But my half-hour was over. Tramp, tramp, came the returning feet; laugh answered to laugh, and an occasional shout awakened the echoes. Saint Katharine, finding me under a tree, congratulated me on my wisdom in lagging behind. The falls were pretty enough, yet hardly worth the climb to those of us who knew the grand New World, where Nature works on so large a scale. Embarking again, we had a good view of Mealfourvornie, an isolated peak rising on the opposite side of the loch, and then swept on our downward way to Fort Augustus, where, by a series of seven locks, we ascend to Aberchalder, at the north end of Loch Oich. The passage of these locks takes an hour or two. For a while we sat upon the deck, watching the slow procedure, as two dozen men tugged and pulled and pushed, turning a sort of turnstile round and round ; and we wondered how long it would have been, in America, before some one of the two dozen would have discovered a way to apply horse or steam power to the work, which was evidently tedious.

Pictures to right of us, pictures to left of us. For our delight, no doubt, even though all unconsciously, a young woman in a brown gown, with a red kerchief knotted about her throat, and no covering on her bright brown hair, had seated herself on the very edge of the canal, and was devoting her strong, supple fingers and all her energies to the making of a great gray fish-net. No royal dame, no princess of the blood, could have glanced at the *canaille* with a more superb scorn than she at us. Her seat was her throne. What cared she for idle tourists? With bagpipes under his arm, his green plaid over his shoulder, and his Scotch cap set jauntily, here comes Sandy, striding along as if in seven-league boots. Two younger laddies — for Sandy is but a lad himself — trot by his side, small copies of the big brother or cousin, bagpipes and all. Scarlet coats gleam here and there, as her Majesty's omnipresent soldiers mingle with the crowd, exchanging greetings and bandying jokes. Old women, in mob-caps with flapping borders, preside at little tables unsheltered from the sun, and dispense beer, ale, milk, and sundry other things to such of the passengers as are tempted to test their hospitality. But the old crones waste no time while waiting. Each has her knitting-work, and the long blue-gray stocking grows apace as the shining needles flash merrily. Children, quaintly dressed, and looking as if they had stepped out of a Kate Greenaway book, race up and down the pier. All is bustle and animation.

Not far off, the monastery of St. Benedict rose in the midst of extensive grounds. We had seen the ghosts of monasteries and abbeys without number, and most entrancing we had found them. Now here was our chance to see one that was alive, — a bit of mediæval existence dropped into the last quarter of the nineteenth century. So climbing the rather long ascent from the dock to the pretty lodge at the entrance of the grounds, we made the usual inquiries of the portress. Yes, we could go in. The fee was a shilling. But it was too late to go over the monastery. A party from the boat had gone up long before (conscientious sight-seers that they were, while we lazily dallied looking at pictures), and there was not time to escort two parties, etc. Overwhelmed with remorse for our shortcomings, we looked at each other in dismay, and were about to go back, when we heard first an unobtrusive call, then a loud shout. Some one at the entrance of the monastery, at a long distance down a gravelled walk, was waving both hands, beckoning frantically, and shouting something that sounded amazingly like a Yankee "Hurry up!"

Hurry we did, to find that the whole party of early birds had been kept waiting all this while, for the possible addition of two or three late comers. Our gesticulating friend, who proved to be the janitor, a talkative, red-haired Irishman, was soon conducting us up stairs and down, from chapel to cloister, from kitchen to refectory, from recitation-room to dormitory. For the monastery of St. Benedict, which was once Fort Augustus, having exchanged the clash of arms for the tumult of cricket and tennis, is now a college, or large school for boys. It was vacation, and not a soul was to be seen, — not a single lad in cap and gown, not so much as the shadow of a black-robed friar in hall, chapter-house, or cloister.

"Where are all the brethren?" asked an inquisitive American, with a broad sombrero and a long beard. "Where do the monks hide themselves? Can't you show 'em up? Come, now, I'll give you an extra shilling."

The janitor looked at him with half-closed eyes, from beneath a pair of heavy eyebrows, for full half a minute. "You won't see them," he said quietly. "The brothers are not such fools as you may think. They're not on exhibition, — the friars."

It was interesting to see a monastery of

our own time. But it lacked the atmosphere, the glamour, the mystery, of the past. It is a fine building, and doubtless a good school. Yet very poor and commonplace did it seem in the strong, clear light of to-day, and very prosaic and shadowless are its brand-new, spick-and-span cloisters, unhallowed by song or legend.

The warning-bell rang sharply, and as we hurried back to the boat we saw one or two tall figures, in black gowns and low, broad-brimmed hats, stealing towards St. Benedict, through the lanes and behind the hedges. Neither the friars nor the monastery were on exhibition now, and the brothers were hastening home.

As we left Fort Augustus we saw the prettiest picture of all. Do the folk about there live out-of-doors, I wonder, French fashion? Soon after we were under way again, on the very shores of the lake, we passed a family group that looked as if posing for a photograph. In the foreground, seated in a low chair, with her knitting in her lap, was a lovely lady in black, whose only head-covering was a widow's cap, so fresh and immaculate that one could but wonder how it was ever made and put on. A younger woman leaned on the back of her chair, and some pretty children, bare-headed, played at her feet, scarcely noticing the steamer as it passed so near them that it would have been easy to toss a ball into the midst of the group. At the right of the fair lady stood a gentleman in full Highland costume, with tartan kilt that left the knees uncovered, a belted jacket, and a bright plaid draped across the breast, and fastened on one shoulder with a cairngorm clasp, or brooch. His richly ornamented sporran, or pouch, reached below the kilt. By his side hung his dirk, and the handle of the sheathed knife with the unpronounceable name, stuck from the top of the stocking, where it is worn. My laird would have been handsome in any costume. In this he was simply superb. For an instant, it seemed like a tableau gotten up for our especial benefit, and I, for one, felt an absurd desire to applaud as the pretty picture faded out of sight.

Soon after we entered Loch Oich it began to rain so violently that we were driven below, much to our chagrin. Yet the passing shower proved to be but a blessing in disguise, and by the time we had passed through two or three more *lochs* and as many *locks* to Banavie, the sun, "clear shining after rain," made the constantly changing panorama more beautiful than before. There we left the steamer, and found omnibuses in waiting to convey us a mile or two across a sort of peninsula to Corpach, where we again embarked.

The long summer afternoon was at its height when we caught our first glimpse of the mighty bulk of Ben Nevis towering above Fort William. A little farther northward stood the round towers of ruined

Castle Inverlochy, once a royal fortress, but dismantled even so long ago as when the chiefs of Glengarry and Keppoch and Lochiel sent the fiery cross far and wide through all the mountains of Lochaber, summoning their vassals to do battle with Montrose against Argyle. Here Argyle had encamped, in the narrow valley " where the Lochy joins Loch Eil," and here Campbells and Camerons, the Knight of Ardenvohr and bold Ranald of the Mist, had met hand to hand in deadly combat. Every mountain pass, every narrow defile, every lonely glen, was peopled with the spirits of the past. And hark! What is that? The bagpipes are sounding. Surely it can be nothing less than the

> "Pibroch of Donuil Dhu,
> Pibroch of Donuil,
> Wake thy wild voice anew,
> Summon Clan Conuil!"

"Wild waves the eagle plume blended with heather," sang he who will live as long as the hills and lakes of his own bonnie Scotland. We saw no eagle plumes that day, but there was not a Scotch man or woman on the boat who did not wear the heather fastened in cap or bonnet. Sometimes it was worn alone, as an all-sufficient ornament; sometimes it was held in place by a great cairngorm, as lustrous and full of imprisoned sunshine as an Oriental topaz, and sometimes by Lochaber axes, dirks, or claymores, fashioned from pebbles set in silver. As a fine contrast to these northern splendours, we had on board an Indian nobleman, Prince Hernam Singh, and his dusky princess, in whose brown ears gleamed long, barbaric pendants of emerald and pearl. All day long, their servant, a tall and stately figure in snowy turban and Oriental costume, stood on one of the stairways leading to the upper deck, silent, impassive, statuesque. He was a most imposing and impressive figure, with his folded arms, his compressed lips, and his dark, inscrutable eyes, that took in every unaccustomed feature of lake and sky and mountain. His master and mistress made few demands upon him; but more than once I saw the latter approach him with a few low words in soft Hindostanee, or perhaps some dainty from the lunch-basket. When we stopped at Corpach, the little street gamins, to say nothing of their elders, crowded about him on the dock; touching his strange garments, peering up into his face, and making themselves generally disagreeable. He did not turn his head nor lift his hand, heeding them no more than if they had been insects buzzing about a marble statue.

Ben Nevis, the highest mountain in Great Britain, is grand and imposing, less from its height, which is only 4406 feet, than from its breadth, if one may use the word. Its circumference at the base is, we were told, nearly twenty-five miles. To the average eye it seems higher than it is, at least when seen from the water. It is a world of precipices, and glens, and huge rents and fissures, and vast shadowy masses that are always taking on new outlines and new proportions. Often it appears in the similitude of some great, crouching monster brooding in sombre majesty over the pygmies at its feet.

At last, as day began to wane, we passed through Loch Aber and the Corran Narrows into Loch Linnhe. And here the mighty spirit of the lakes and mountains took possession of us all, and held that boat-load of merry people silent and spellbound. It was as if we were being borne onward, swiftly and noiselessly, into the inmost holy of holies. Even the captain and the very deck-hands stood like men entranced, overwhelmed by the surpassing splendour. Anything so grand, so weird, so magical, can hardly be imagined, much less described. The rain of two hours before had left the air heavy with vapour, through which the sun now shone gloriously, producing the most marvellous effects. "You might make this trip a hundred times, ladies," said the captain, as he stood uncovered, "and not get the half of what you are getting to-day,—no, nor the tenth of it."

I quote this, lest some of our dear, wandering kinsfolk, who have been "down the Caledonia Canal" on some dull, gray day, when the Scotch mists hemmed them in on all sides, and they could scarcely see beyond the decks, should cry out, "How that woman exaggerates!" But we have all seen transformation scenes on the stage, where the effect of light and colour, of rapidly dissolving views, and of seemingly supernatural revelations filled us with wordless awe. Now make the stage one vast panorama of shining, sparkling water, as still as a sheet of silver. Dot the surface with islands, dark masses of verdure rising out of the depths, and often picturesquely beautiful with ivy-grown mouldering towers, broken arches, and here and there a stately monument. Let the nearer hills, sloping upwards from the shores, be cultivated and clothed with living green more than half-way up; make them gentle and homelike by building stately mansions on the broad terraces, and letting small gray cottages, like birds'-nests, perch on the sightly cliffs; then, stretching far above these human habitations, let the purple of the wild heather, blending with the soft olives of ferns and mosses, climb to their very tops. Beyond them, tier on tier, not in regular ranges, but jutting out edgewise, and crosswise, and *all*wise, let the mightier hills stretch upwards and onwards, appearing and disappearing; now looming up out of the vapour in cold, blue splendour, then suddenly vanishing like pallid ghosts; changing every moment; presenting constantly new vistas, new cloud marvels, and new openings into far, radiant reaches,

s

through which you seem to see heaven itself. Throw over all this light veils of mist, that soften rather than obscure, — pale gray, dazzling silver, soft rose, translucent amber, purple amethyst, — veils that float, and lift, and waver, with every breath and with every motion of the boat, and you will have some faint idea of what our eyes beheld that August evening as we crossed Loch Linnhe and passed into Loch Leven, pausing for a few moments at Ballachulish, and then, turning into Linnhe again, swept on our downward way towards Oban. But you must do still more. You must imagine all this magnificence of cloud and mountain and island so perfectly mirrored in the clear, still waters of the lake that even the changing splendour of colour was duplicated, and heaven was below as well as above us.

It grew dark and chill at last. The overpowering glory died, and earth was earth once more. But the effect remained.

Young men and maidens, old men and children, were content to sit in silence, or to speak in subdued whispers, as we watched for the first gleam of the semicircular cordon of lights that guard the bay of Oban.

THE END.

THE WORKS OF WILLIAM WINTER.

SHAKESPEARE'S ENGLAND. Library Edition. Illustrated. 12mo. Cloth. $2.00. Pocket Edition. 18mo. Cloth. 75 cents. Miniature Edition. 18mo. Paper. 25 cents.

GRAY DAYS AND GOLD: In England and Scotland. Pocket Edition. 18mo. Cloth. 75 cents.

OLD SHRINES AND IVY: Containing Shrines of History and Shrines of Literature. Pocket Edition. 18mo. Cloth. 75 cents.

WANDERERS: Being The Poems of William Winter. Pocket Edition. With a Portrait of the Author. 18mo. Cloth. 75 cents.

SHADOWS OF THE STAGE. Three Volumes. First Series. 1893. 18mo. Cloth. 75 cents. Second Series. 1893. 18mo. Cloth. 75 cents. Third Series. 1895. 18mo. Cloth. 75 cents.

LIFE AND ART OF EDWIN BOOTH. Pocket Edition. With a New and Rare Portrait of Booth as Hamlet. 18mo. Cloth. 75 cents. Miniature Edition. 18mo. Paper. 25 cents.

LIFE AND ART OF JOSEPH JEFFERSON. Library Edition. 12mo. With SIXTEEN FULL-PAGE ILLUSTRATIONS; Portraits of Jefferson in Character, etc. Cloth. $2.25. This volume contains a full account of Jefferson's ancestors upon the stage, and covers a period of more than 160 years in Dramatic History—from 1728 to 1894.

ORATIONS BY WILLIAM WINTER. Two Volumes. **George William Curtis.** A Commemorative Oration, Delivered before the People of Staten Island, at the Castleton, St. George, February 24, 1893. 18mo. Cloth. 50 cents.

The Press and the Stage. An Oration in Reply to Dion Boucicault. Delivered at the Brunswick, N.Y., before the Goethe Society, January 28, 1889. Limited Edition, on Hand-made Paper. 12mo. Cloth. $1.50.

IN PREPARATION.

BROWN HEATH AND BLUE BELLS: Being Sketches of Scotland. With Other Papers.

UNIFORM WITH THIS VOLUME.

AMIEL'S JOURNAL.

The Journal Intime of Henri-Frédéric Amiel.

TRANSLATED, WITH AN INTRODUCTION AND NOTES.
WITH A PORTRAIT.

New Edition. 2 Vols. 18mo. $1.50.

"A wealth of thought and a power of expression which would make the fortune of a dozen less able works." — *Churchman.*

"A work of wonderful beauty, depth, and charm. . . . Will stand beside such confessions as St. Augustine's and Pascal's. . . . It is a book to converse with again and again; fit to stand among the choicest volumes that we esteem as friends of our souls." — *Christian Register.*

MACMILLAN & CO.,
66 FIFTH AVENUE, NEW YORK.

UNIFORM WITH THIS VOLUME.

THE
FRIENDSHIP OF NATURE.

A NEW ENGLAND CHRONICLE OF BIRDS AND FLOWERS.

Cloth, 18mo, Gilt Top, 75 cts. Large Paper Edition, with Illustrations, $3.00.

"A charming chronicle it is, abounding in excellent descriptions and interesting comment." — *Chicago Evening Journal.*

"The author sees and vividly describes what she sees. But more, she has rare insight and sees deeply, and the most precious things lie deep." — *Boston Daily Advertiser.*

"There is much of the feeling of Henry D. Thoreau between the covers of this book, and the expression is characterized by a poetic appreciation of the value of word-combination which is admirable." — *Philadelphia Evening Bulletin.*

"A delightful little book, . . . which brings one into intimate acquaintance with nature, the wild flowers, the fields, and the brooks." — *Springfield Union.*

"Thoroughly delightful reading." — *Boston Courier.*
"A very clever little book. It . . . takes us through a New England year, describing the birds, flowers, and woods in a most poetical and delightful mood." — *Detroit Free Press.*

MACMILLAN & CO.,
66 FIFTH AVENUE, NEW YORK.

UNIFORM WITH THIS VOLUME.

A New Handy-Volume Edition.

THE MAKERS OF FLORENCE.

DANTE, GIOTTO, SAVONAROLA, AND THEIR CITY.

By MRS. OLIPHANT.

With Portrait of Savonarola, and sixty Illustrations from Drawings from Professor DELAMOTTE, and many page plates reproduced from pictures by Florentine artists. In 4 volumes, 18mo, $3.00; each volume sold separately, 75 cents each.

THE NOVEL:
WHAT IT IS.

By F. MARION CRAWFORD,

Author of "Children of the King," "A Roman Singer," "Saracinesca," etc.

With Photogravure Portrait of the Author.

18mo. Cloth. 75 cents.

PARABLES FROM NATURE.

By MRS. ALFRED GATTY,

Author of "Aunt Judy's Tales," etc.

In 2 vols. 18mo. $1.50.

MACMILLAN & CO.,
66 FIFTH AVENUE, NEW YORK.

UNIVERSITY of CALIFORNIA
AT
LOS ANGELES
LIBRARY

www.ingramcontent.com/pod-product-compliance
Lightning Source LLC
Chambersburg PA
CBHW031252250426
43672CB00029BA/2226